Reforming the Welfare

Reforming the Welfare

The politics of change in the personal social services

Phoebe Hall

HEINEMANN
LONDON

Heinemann Educational Books Ltd
LONDON EDINBURGH MELBOURNE AUCKLAND TORONTO
HONG KONG SINGAPORE KUALA LUMPUR NEW DELHI
NAIROBI JOHANNESBURG LUSAKA IBADAN
KINGSTON

ISBN 0 435 82400 7

© Phoebe Hall 1976
First published 1976

Published by Heinemann Educational Books Ltd.,
48 Charles Street, London W1X 8AH

Printed and bound in Great Britain by Morrison and Gibb Ltd.,
London and Edinburgh

Contents

TO MY PARENTS

Acknowledgements

Most research projects are dependent upon the help and encouragement of many people but perhaps studies of 'current history' rely even more heavily upon the goodwill of others. Certainly, this book could never have been written without the help of academics, civil servants, politicians and practitioners. They are too numerous to mention here but a list of the main contributors is given in Appendix Four.

The Joseph Rowntree Memorial Trust very kindly financed the study and Bristol University were good enough to administer it. Much of the research took place in London and hence I needed a room and library facilities there; I would like to thank the National Institute for Social Work for providing me with these. The penultimate draft was written whilst I was a Research Fellow at the Centre for Studies in Social Policy where many of the staff gave me helpful suggestions. I am particularly grateful to Rudolf Klein for his comments on early drafts and the very valuable advice and encouragement he gave.

I interviewed all the members of the committee (with the exception of the late Sir Charles Barratt) and, without their co-operation and indulgence, much of the detail of the committee's functioning would have been lost. I am especially grateful to Lord Seebohm, Lady Serota and Robin Huws Jones for their factual contributions to the study and their help on early drafts of the manuscript.

Professor Roy Parker obtained the financial backing for the project and has subsequently been a constant source of support. As a member of the committee he was able to fill in some of the gaps in my knowledge and has provided me with many useful leads. I should like to thank my husband, Tony, for his generous help, both in the interpretation of the data and in revisions to the final draft. Lastly, my thanks are due to Mrs Eve Shields, who bore the brunt of the secretarial work, spending many tedious evenings typing the manuscript.

I must emphasize that, despite my reliance upon the experience of others, the opinions expressed here and the defects of the work are entirely mine.

Phoebe Hall,
Bristol University
October 1975

Introduction

This study looks at attempts during the 1960s to grapple with the vastly complex questions of which social welfare services to make available, to whom and how. Throughout the fifties many of those involved in providing social work and related services appeared content to work within, or modify only marginally, the constraints imposed by decisions put into effect in 1948. However, by the early sixties these constraints were rapidly becoming unacceptable and, although at first they were poorly articulated, the demands for change grew throughout the decade.

These pressures for a reappraisal of local authority welfare services culminated in the passing of the Local Authority Social Services Act, 1970, which required local authorities to create a new committee and to appoint a director in charge of a 'social services department'. These new committees were to take over services which had previously been the responsibility of a variety of local committees, namely those of the welfare and children's committees, and certain duties from the health, education and housing committees.

The purpose of this study is to examine the processes which lay behind the creation of these new departments and behind other equally important changes. The Social Services Act was accompanied by a number of related developments such as the expansion of social work activities of all kinds, a re-examination of the function and nature of social work, the emergence of a new professional identity amongst social workers and changes in their training. In its emphasis on the processes of change it is hoped that the study will appeal not only to those interested in social work but also to students of political processes and policy development.

Two points must be made at the outset. First, we are considering what have come to be called 'the personal social services'. The term itself is fairly new; in 1965 a committee of enquiry [1] chaired by Lord Seebohm was asked to examine these services but it experienced great

difficulty in being precise about their essential nature.[1] Rather than
define their common qualities, the committee preferred to use a
functional definition. It took as its 'starting point' the whole of the
work of the children's and welfare departments and social work elements
in the health, education and housing departments. These services
formed the core of the personal social services with others such as
probation and the social work elements within the National Assistance
Board on the periphery. Roughly, then, these are the social services
under review here.

Second, any study of change is bound to involve some rationalization
about the course of events. It is tempting for the researcher to produce
a tidy explanation from a mass of complex, often conflicting, evidence.
One of the advantages of current history is the opportunity it affords for
recording the accounts of the individuals involved. But these accounts
differ. Sometimes the difference is marginal in that the emphasis placed
upon events, issues and key personalities varies; sometimes it is significant in that completely conflicting versions are given. Since it is often
impossible to verify 'the facts', the researcher has to recount these
differences or attempt to synthesize them. As this study progressed, I
found a considerable disparity of view as to what were the key events
which led to the formation of the social services departments and as far
as possible these variations have been discussed in the text.

The story was an exciting one to piece together since, contrary to the
views of some observers, it was by no means a straightforward and
predictable policy development. In retrospect, and without detailed
knowledge of a policy's fortunes, it is often easy to interpret the results
of a decision-making process as the logical, almost inevitable outcome
of pressures to reform the existing system. Looking back at the planning
of the personal social services from the mid-sixties onwards, it may
seem that the Seebohm Committee merely undertook the administrative work of outlining a detailed blueprint and that, thereafter, the
government simply converted the main points of the report into a Bill
which was then duly agreed and passed. As this study progressed,
however, it became clear that the final outcome of the policy-making
process could very easily have been different.

The Seebohm Committee was composed of members with a wide
diversity of experience, whose views on the matters in hand varied
considerably at the outset. Moreover, they had to process a large
amount of evidence which propounded a number of very different

[1] The term appears to have been coined for the committee. I can find no
reference to it in the literature prior to 1965.

solutions. There was powerful opposition to the committee's chosen solution from some civil servants and politicians, medical pressure groups and most of the local authority associations. By contrast, the main supporters of the committee's conclusions were a newly emergent, diverse and politically inexperienced lobby—the social workers. The Cabinet's reception of the committee's report was very unfavourable and Crossman, Secretary of State for Social Services, was far from convinced by its arguments. The report caused dissension among senior Labour ministers by requesting that one central government department should take responsibility for the reorganized services, a reform which could denude either the D.H.S.S. (headed by Crossman) or the Home Office (whose Secretary of State was Callaghan) of important services. Furthermore, the reorganization of the personal social services had to compete for the attention of the public, the civil servants, and pressure groups with other policies under consideration; namely the reorganization of the National Health Service, the planning and implementation of educational priority areas, local government reorganization, a new pensions plan and modified strategies for the treatment of young offenders. Given such difficulties, it is perhaps surprising that the 1970 Social Services Act survived in any form whatsoever. The task of studying the reorganization is therefore not simply that of chronicling the events and describing the exact shape of the final legislation, but the far more difficult one of explaining why these changes happened at all.

Chapter One examines the general trends which led to the request for a committee of enquiry in the mid-sixties. It involves looking briefly at past structures for delivering services to those in need, at the extent to which problems were seen as structural ones, at the difficulties observers and practitioners saw thrown up by the administrative boundaries then in operation and at the solutions put forward. The proposal with the widest support gained considerable momentum during the early sixties and came close to being included in a white paper. Chapter Two looks at the reasons why such a scheme was shelved and at the demand for and opposition to a committee of enquiry. The formation of a committee was more contentious than many students realize. Why was such machinery necessary and what were the effects of ambivalent attitudes towards an enquiry on its terms of reference and choice of membership?

In defining the problems of the social work services in the mid-sixties and selecting a solution the Seebohm Committee was quite crucial. Chapter Three examines the task the enquiry set itself, its definition of the problems, its early difficulties and the importance of evidence and research. It covers such questions as which interest groups were involved and their strategies if any. How effectively did certain organizations put their cases? Where were the major alliances and conflicts? Chapter Four is concerned with the committee's conclusions and the interplay of members' views, evidence and research in the formation of decisions. At this stage considerations include the predictability of the report (given the membership, terms of reference, evidence, research and so on) and its presentation.

Chapter Five examines the impact of the committee's work, its unfriendly political reception, pressure group efforts to secure a commitment to reorganization and the reasons for the eventual acceptance of the committee's main proposals. The penultimate chapter covers the final period during which pressure group activity was at its fiercest. It looks at some groups' efforts to influence the shape of the impending reorganization by modifying their tactics. In forming the Social Services Act, 1970, which were the key issues and how were these resolved? Chapter Seven discusses the formation of the social services department in more general terms, applying concepts first used in an earlier study by myself and others [2]. Clearly, the usual reservations regarding the use of case-study material must be made [3]. There are strict limits on the general applicability of the conclusions but, bearing these in mind, the last chapter draws out some of the more significant decisions and examines the factors which influenced them.

1 General Pressures for Change

One Welfare Service or Several?

Before considering post-war decisions and their influence on recent policy concerning the social work and related services, a brief excursion into Poor Law history will demonstrate the intractable nature of some of the issues involved. Under the Poor Law of 1834 services for various groups requiring assistance—children, the old, the sick, the handicapped and the delinquent—were administered by a single local agency, the Poor Law Union, under the direction of Poor Law Guardians and through the medium of the workhouse. As the only public authority providing assistance to the pauper, the union was inevitably a multi-purpose organization and many felt that it failed to create the variety of approaches appropriate to the heterogeneous group for which it catered. Requests for greater differentiation in the treatment of various groups in need were made long before the Royal Commission on the Poor Laws was established in 1905 but the issues were discussed in depth and set out particularly clearly in its publications.

The Minority Report of the Commission [1] suggested that the general mixed workhouse should be abolished and that services for different groups of destitute persons should be administratively separate. Services which were at that time provided for the pauper by the destitution authorities should, it argued, be provided by the county and county borough councils. Children of school age should be transferred to the education committee. The sick, the permanently incapacitated, infants under school age and the elderly requiring institutional care should become the responsibility of the health committee, the mentally defective that of the asylums committee and the aged in receipt of pensions that of the pensions committee. These committees, it maintained, should be put under the aegis of a single government department. The overriding concern of the minority group was to improve the standard of these services, and they believed that the separation of responsibilities for services to different groups and the development of specialist skills by the staff involved was the best solution. This was despite the difficulties it might present for a family with multiple problems.

The Majority Report opposed this view on grounds very similar to those used by the critics of the structure obtaining during the nineteen-fifties and sixties and those later deployed by the Seebohm Committee.

> The question at issue [it argued] is whether the work of maintaining those members of the community who have lost their economic independence can safely be entrusted to authorities whose primary duty is something quite distinct—such as that of Education or Sanitation—or whether it is essential that there should be an authority devoting itself entirely to the work . . . What is needed is a disinterested authority, practised in looking at all sides of a question and able to call on skilled assistance. The specialist is too apt to see only what interests him in the first instance and to disregard wider issues . . . Such separation [it maintained] must result in a multiplication of inquiries and visitations, causing annoyance and waste of time and money. Administrative inefficiency and confusion [and] delay and friction would be unavoidable [2].

The minority group recognized the difficulties that their solution might present for the family with multiple problems. 'There is the objection,' they stated, 'that the breaking up of the Poor Law involves the breaking up of the family. There is the objection that the proposed scheme would lead to the harassing of the poor in their own homes by a multiplicity of officers, each bent on enforcing his own conditions' [3]. Acknowledging the need for co-ordinating machinery if their suggestion were put into effect, the group proposed that a Registrar for each local authority area should be appointed and that he should be responsible for maintaining a register of all those in receipt of assistance. He would, therefore, be in a position to check whether members of one family were obtaining aid from several authorities at once. This proposal, along with the rest of the scheme, was never accepted. In their deliberations, however, the Commission had faced one of the major problems which subsequently confronted the Seebohm Committee; a single administrative unit providing services for a variety of groups avoids the difficulties of inter-agency co-ordination but at the expense of firm differentiation between categories of need, and possibly also at the expense of improving overall standards.

Comprehensive reorganization of welfare and assistance provisions did not take place until the mid-forties by which time their haphazard growth had created considerable administrative confusion. The destitution authorities continued to exist until 1948, although the functions of the Poor Law Guardians were transferred to counties and county boroughs in 1929. Services for the old remained largely institutional, few domiciliary welfare services being developed by local authorities until after 1948. The same was true for the physically and mentally handicapped although institutional care for these groups improved somewhat. Services for deprived and neglected children were divided between several authorities; the local destitution, health and education committees all had responsibilities in this area. Besides a range of statutory provisions there were the services of a host of voluntary organizations [4].

The Structure of Welfare Services in 1948

Most social policies are not innovatory but evolutionary. Few policies break entirely new ground, the majority being a recasting of the satisfactory aspects of existing legislation and practice or a reaction to the problems created by past policies or earlier inaction. The creation of the social services departments was, in part, a reaction to the problems arising from the inadequacies of the administrative structures established in 1946–8.

Until 1970 the structure of the local authority welfare services was based upon three pieces of legislation passed after the second world war. The Children Act, 1948, provided for 'a comprehensive service for the care of children who have not the benefit of a normal home life'. The National Health Service Act, which came into operation in 1948, placed certain powers and duties upon local health departments such as maternity and child welfare services, services for the mentally ill and subnormal, together with home nursing, health visiting and home helps. The National Assistance Act, 1948, laid the foundations of the local authority welfare department's services by making the county and county borough councils responsible for providing accommodation and other services for the elderly, the physically handicapped and the homeless.

Services for deprived children [5]

In March 1945 the central government departments responsible for the welfare of children set up a committee, under the chairmanship of

Dame Myra Curtis, 'to inquire into existing methods of providing for children who from loss of parents or from any cause whatever are deprived of a normal home life with their own parents or relatives; and to consider what further measures should be taken to ensure that these children are brought up under conditions best calculated to compensate them for lack of parental care' [6]. Although they acknówledged it as an important matter, the enquiry excluded consideration of the neglect of children in their own homes. This issue was to assume much greater proportions in the decades which followed.

The committee's report, produced after only eighteen months, did not mince its words, providing a graphic description of the poor conditions under which children 'in care' were being brought up. Criticisms were levelled at both the low standards of institutional care and at grossly unsatisfactory boarding-out arrangements. At times very reminiscent of its important predecessor, the Royal Commission on the Poor Laws, the Curtis Report pointed to divided responsibilities as one of the main underlying problems resulting in confusion, lack of co-ordination and inconsistency of treatment.

According to the characteristics of a child and the circumstances under which he came to the attention of the authorities, he might become the responsibility of any one of five central government departments (Ministry of Health, Home Office, Ministry of Pensions, Board of Control or Ministry of Education) or any of three local government committees (Public Assistance Committee, Health Committee or Education Committee). He might, alternatively, be taken in by one of the plethora of voluntary organizations which existed at this time to supplement the chaotic and inadequate facilities provided by the state.

The Curtis Committee's proposed solution to the administrative confusion, delay and variation in standards, which they attributed in part to these divisions of responsibility, was unification. Overall responsibility for deprived children should, they argued, be vested in one central government department 'which would define and maintain standards by inspection, advice and direction'. Service provision would be the responsibility of the local authorities. Each county and county borough council should be required to appoint a children's committee with its own chief officer to head a new children's department.

Health and welfare services

The Curtis Report was a milestone in the history of services for deprived children. It provided a charter which not only outlined the organization structure of post-war services, but also provided a well argued, coherent rationale for changes in the residential care and boarding-out arrangements for children. Unfortunately, for all concerned, no such charter prescribed the future of welfare services for other categories of people in need. Whilst the principle of unification was being propounded for children, a similar approach was not applied to the structure of services for groups such as the elderly and the handicapped. Although the National Assistance Act carried the words 'The existing Poor Law shall cease to have effect', it did little but reallocate elements of the Poor Law regime to different agencies. Responsibility for financial assistance for those in need after 1948 was to be that of the National Assistance Board; responsibility for domiciliary and residential help in kind was that of the county and county borough councils. The absence of any major rethinking of the type of care to be provided is reflected in the residential orientation of the provisions for the care of the elderly. Local authorities were given two primary duties. First, to provide residential accommodation 'for persons who by reasons of age, infirmity or any other circumstances are in need of care or attention which is not otherwise available to them'. Second, to provide temporary accommodation in situations of urgent need 'in circumstances which could not reasonably have been foreseen or in such circumstances as the local authority may in a particular case determine' [7]. The contrast with the community care orientation of the children's services is striking. Here, residential provision was only provided as a last resort where boarding out was not possible. In addition to these two duties, local authorities were empowered to provide services for the blind, deaf, dumb and general classes of handicap in residential, semi-residential or domiciliary settings. They were also allowed to employ voluntary organizations as agents for providing facilities for both the elderly and the handicapped —a provision used both to extend residential accommodation and provide domiciliary services such as meals on wheels. All of these functions, and a range of other detailed regulations and supervisory activities, were to be performed 'under the general guidance of the minister' and in accordance with the provisions and regulations made by him.

The National Assistance Act has since been heavily criticized for its very narrow focus and limited vision. 'The Act,' writes Julia Parker, 'was a feeble instrument for such a grand design. Many of the powers it conferred upon local authorities were permissive; all the emphasis was on residential accommodation; there was no clear guidance about the development of welfare services; little thought had been given to the .

sort of staff that would be needed for the developing services; and no attention was paid to the local administrative arrangements. In short, the local authorities were left with limited powers and little guidance to develop their services as they felt inclined or able' [8].

The National Health Service Act, 1946, complicated an already elaborate and confused picture still further. Not only did it create a tripartite structure for the National Health Service—differentiating between the hospital service, the general practitioner service and environmental health services of the local authorities—but it vested the last with responsibilities which cut across the boundaries with other social welfare departments. Under the Act the health departments of county and county borough councils were given a statutory duty to provide health centres and ambulances; services for expectant and nursing mothers and children under five; midwives, health visitors and home nurses, and to arrange for vaccination and immunization against smallpox and diphtheria. In addition, local authorities were given the powers to undertake preventive work, to provide care and after-care for the ill or mentally defective; and to provide home help services for those in special need.

The organizational structure of local authority health and welfare services was no less complicated than the division of responsibilities between the three main welfare departments. Under the 1948 National Assistance Act, county and county borough councils were required to establish a committee for the discharge of their functions under Part III of the Act. However, subject to the approval of the Minister of Health, these functions could be transferred to some other committee of the local authority. Further, under the Local Government Act, 1958, county and county boroughs could delegate these functions, with the exception of the duty to provide residential accommodation, to borough or urban districts with a population of 60,000 or more. By 1968, the national picture was again chaotic. One hundred and twenty-nine authorities had a welfare committee with sole responsibility for welfare services; in twenty-eight these services were provided by the health committee, and a further eighteen authorities had combined health and welfare departments. In some authorities even where there was a clear distinction between the health and the welfare committees, there was no equally clear distinction between health and welfare services. For example, the health committee rather than the welfare committee might be responsible for services for the handicapped [9].

In addition to these major provisions, other local authority departments developed welfare services because of their own special needs.

Education departments provided special education facilities for the handicapped, education welfare services, including arrangements for enforcing school attendance, for providing free meals and clothing, and educational maintenance allowances. They were also responsible for the school health services, including child guidance, and the youth, and youth employment services. Local authority housing departments had also come to contain a strong welfare element as the numbers of people they accommodated increased and as policies were developed for slum clearance, redevelopment and the consequent rehousing of increasingly large numbers of families.

At central government level the pattern of divided responsibility was much the same. The Ministry of Health was responsible for those services administered by local health and welfare departments, the Home Office for children's departments and the juvenile court system, the Ministry of Housing for local welfare services and the Ministry of Education for those of local authority education departments.

Pressures for Change

The inadequacies of the boundaries surrounding our welfare agencies came under growing pressure as the nineteen-fifties progressed. Ideas concerning the nature of social need, and hence the proper focus for social work, altered. The services in question expanded very rapidly, increasing costs and putting greater emphasis on the need for effective planning machinery. A sense of common identity developed amongst social workers and, as it did so, the pressure for reorganization of the services within which they worked increased.

The growth of social welfare services

During the fifties, for Whitehall perhaps the most crucial feature of the local authority social welfare services was their rapid expansion. The consequent growth in expenditure brought the welfare services into the spotlight as never before. The amount spent on the care of children in need, the aged, the handicapped and the homeless rose considerably after 1948. In the United Kingdom, total expenditure on child care and local welfare services increased by almost 180% (at constant prices) between 1952 and 1968. As can be seen in Table 1 this growth was particularly rapid in the local welfare services, for the elderly and handicapped, but both child care and welfare expenditure far outstripped the general rise in total public expenditure. These increases largely reflect real changes in the range and quality of services provided, but are partly accounted for by more fundamental changes in demography. For example, between 1951 and 1971 the number of elderly

Table 1   Growth in Selected Areas of Public Expenditure, 1952–68
At 1971–2 out-turn prices

	1952	1960	1968	Total growth, 1952–68 %
		£m		
Military defence	3,440	2,728	3,104	−9·8
Public protection[1]	247	347	627	+153·8
Housing and environment	1,496	1,363	2,479	+65·7
Education	957	1,532	2,765	+188·9
Health[2]	1,100	1,441	2,142	+94·7
Social security	1,720	2,486	4,181	+143·1
Child care	37	43	84	+127·0
Local welfare services	35	54	117	+234·3
Total public expenditure	13,932	15,626	24,221	+73·9
Gross national product (at factor cost)	29,639	37,049	46,818	+58·0

[1] Comprises Police, Prisons, Parliament and Law Courts, Fire Services.
[2] All sectors of the National Health Services, including local authority health services.
Source: Derived from Sir Samuel Goldman, *Public Expenditure, Management and Control,* H.M.S.O., 1973, pp. 63–71.

people[1] in the United Kingdom increased from 6,850,000 to 8,898,000 —almost 30%. In 1951 the elderly represented 13.6% of the total population; by 1971 they accounted for 16% [10].

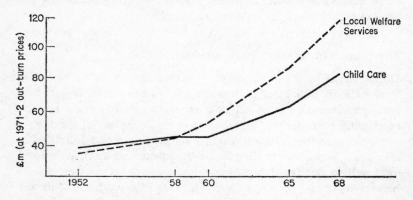

Source: Derived from Sir Samuel Goldman, *Public Expenditure, Management and Control,* H.M.S.O., 1973, p. 69.

[1] Includes men aged at least 65 and women aged at least 60.

The growth in expenditure throughout this period was not uniform. As can be seen in Figure 1, the most dramatic increases date from the late 1950s and early 1960s. This was largely the result of a considerable increase in the levels of capital expenditure, and the revenue consequences of this investment, particularly for the care of the elderly. Capital expenditure on local welfare services tripled between 1958 and 1965, as compared with a more modest 83% rise in current expenditure; capital expenditure on child care doubled, whilst revenue expenditure increased by only 13.2% [11].

Inadequate planning machinery

As these social welfare services became big business, concern over their organization and effectiveness grew but the machinery for policy development failed to keep pace. The division of responsibility for them created barriers both at central and local government levels which were often acknowledged but seldom overcome. Within Whitehall, the split of welfare functions between two major government departments—the Home Office and the Ministry of Health—precluded the possibility of planning across the board. A large number of departmental committees looked at aspects of social work and related fields but their terms of reference never transcended departmental boundaries [12]. Attempts were made, when discussing the possibility of an enquiry in 1956, to create a committee responsible to both the Home Office and the Ministry of Health with a brief encompassing the welfare services of both departments but agreement could not be reached.

Nevertheless, despite their narrow focus, the enquiries of the fifties and early sixties addressed themselves to issues which later became important factors both in the creation of the Seebohm Committee and in subsequent debates on alternative models for the reorganization of the personal social services. Some of their contributions will be discussed in the following pages.

New approaches in social work

For many years after the introduction of the Poor Law Amendment Act in 1834, social need continued to be seen primarily as the consequence of individual failure. Naturally, therefore, the focus of attention when treating social ills was the individual and the separation of that individual from his family and community context. Hence the predominance of institutions of one sort and another—from the workhouse to the asylum. This approach, as we have seen, was largely discarded in the reappraisal of the children's services during and immediately after the war, but it remained a central feature of welfare services for other groups. From the late nineteen-forties onwards, however, these assumptions were increasingly called into question. Emphasis upon individual incapacity as the cause of social problems gave way to a greater stress upon social or family pressures. The focus of intervention, therefore, shifted from the individual in isolation, to the individual within his immediate and wider environment. Parallel movements in both the children's and health and welfare services were the result of this new perspective. In the children's services it influenced the move towards greater prevention; in health and welfare it was the driving force behind arguments for community care. These trends were reflected in the departmental enquiries of the period.

As the nature of social work was examined more closely [13] greater emphasis was placed upon the need to prevent social ills rather than merely treat the symptoms. The Younghusband Report recognized the problem and maintained that:

> The need to help . . . families is most easily seen in acute situations, if there is neglect or ill-treatment of children, or if the family is likely to break up from other causes. There is a similar or perhaps greater need to recognise the potential problem before it becomes acute, and to provide help to any family known to health or welfare departments which is in difficulties or where some special need arises [14].

The Ingleby Committee was more specifically concerned with prevention; the prevention of juvenile crime. Its terms of reference were to examine the juvenile courts and approved school system and to make recommendations on whether local authorities responsible for child care should 'be given new powers and duties to prevent or forestall the suffering of children through neglect in their own homes'. Answering the second part of their terms of reference, the committee proposed that children's departments should be given a general duty and greater powers to carry out preventive work and that they should be able to provide for material needs which could not be met from other sources. In 1963, The Children and Young Persons Act was passed, putting these suggestions into effect, thereby strengthening the ability of children's departments to forestall family problems.

Allied to the accent upon prevention was an emphasis on the desirability of providing care in a community or family setting. The reaction against the use of large, inhuman institutions for the care of long-stay patients has been well documented [15]. It captured particular attention during the fifties with regard to the treatment of the mentally handicapped. The Royal Commission on Mental Illness and Mental Deficiency stated in 1957 that

> It is not now generally considered in the best interests of patients who are fit to live in the general community that they should be in large or remote institutions such as the present mental illness and mental deficiency hospitals [16].

Adopting this approach meant thinking seriously about the scale and quality of community services and their capacity to shoulder the increased demand for services. The Mental Health Act of 1959 placed a duty upon local authorities to provide community services for the mentally ill and subnormal, and the approach spread quickly to the treatment of other groups. The Hospital Plan of 1962 [17] estimated the future demand for hospital beds on the basis that provision would be made only for those who could not be cared for within the community. In the Health and Welfare Plans produced the following year [18] local authorities attempted to face up to the challenge presented by this emphasis upon community services but the need for a more fundamental reappraisal was gradually being recognized.

Accompanying the arguments that prevention and community care were socially desirable were claims that such approaches made sense economically. The Younghusband Committee, for instance, put the case for a preventive approach in both social and financial terms, arguing that 'failure to give effective help in time frequently results in a demand for more costly services' [19].

A common identity amongst social workers

Accompanying debates about developments in social welfare was the emergence of a feeling of common identity amongst the staff working within those services. The formation of any professional group depends upon establishing a core of common knowledge and, if one takes the model of the medical profession, this is then followed by an attempt to develop specializations. For social workers, the first of these processes began in the mid-thirties when a formal attempt was made to bring together social workers of differing backgrounds and training [20].

The British Federation of Social Workers was created in 1936, the prime movers being psychiatric social workers who had a well-established professional association of their own composed of relatively highly trained social workers. The federation, which had sixteen constituent associations, concentrated mainly on training. A report of its training committee in 1942 stressed the need for an enquiry into common elements in the education and background of social workers. It was becoming clear by the end of the 1940s, however, that the unification of social workers could not be pursued successfully through a federal system, some of whose members were primarily concerned to protect their own standards of training. Moreover, the federation was dependent upon the financial contributions of its member organizations. In 1949, therefore, the constitution was modified to make individual membership the main basis of the federation but allowing the associations to affiliate and to retain a representative on the council, in return for a small subscription. From 1949 to 1951 the British Federation of Social Workers was gradually modified, changing its name in the process to the Association of Social Workers, a professional body composed of individuals committed to the pursuit of a unified profession. The early years of the association were difficult ones, much of its time being devoted to considering ways of improving the professional basis of social work; a Working Party to investigate the possibility of forming a register of social workers was established.

Registration was not implemented, as the Working Party suggested, but other efforts by the association bore fruit. The first generic (general) social work course—the Applied Social Studies Course started at the London School of Economics in 1954—was in part the result of pressure by the Association of Social Workers to introduce a common basis to the training of all social workers.

In 1959 a Joint Training Council for Social Work, representing nine professional social work bodies, was formed but it was superseded in 1963 by the Standing Conference of Organisations of Social Workers, which was composed of eight groups [21]. Its concerns were wider than training alone. The conference was formed at a crucial stage in the development of ideas concerning social work. By 1966, when the Seebohm Committee asked for evidence on the reorganization of local social services, many of the key social work organizations had had three years in which to discuss their views on the future of their profession. This is not to say that no conflicts emerged. Analysis of their evidence to the committee reveals important differences of opinion but the fact that a common core to their proposals existed was of great importance.

The concern of social workers themselves with their role and training was complemented by the important contribution of two committees which examined these issues from the perspective of the client as well as that of the profession. A Working Party, established to consider the role, training and recruitment of health visitors, paid particular attention to the question of specialization by welfare staff.

We deprecate specialisation [it announced] because it narrows the field of interest, complicates family visiting, reduces the opportunity for service by the general duties staff and thus lessens the attractiveness of the profession. Much of what is now specialised could be incorporated in general duties. If specialisation is unavoidable . . . staff should, if possible, retain a small area for general duties purposes or return from time to time to general duties work [22].

The role of the social worker and the desirable degree of specialization were taken much further by the Younghusband Committee whose remit covered social workers in the whole of the health and welfare services (but not the children's services). One of its main recommendations was that

the focus of social work should be on the social and personal needs of the family rather than a particular aspect of the problem. In our view less specialised functions would provide a better service and make a more profitable use of the resources available [23].

The Younghusband Committee was concerned also with training and did not miss the opportunity to suggest courses which would emphasize the generic elements within social work. We have seen that such generic courses were not entirely new but they expanded much more rapidly following the publication of the report. As a result of the committee's recommendations, a Council for Training in Social Work was created in 1962 which awarded the Certificate in Social Work for those completing a two-year generic training.[1] The same year another of the Younghusband Committee's suggestions, the creation of an academic body to develop social work training, was implemented when the National Institute for Social Work Training was formed.[2]

As common skills were defined, so the administrative divisions separating social workers came into question. If social workers practised

[1] Provision for the council was made in the Health Visiting and Social Work (Training) Act, 1962.

[2] The Institute's first Principal was Robin Huws Jones, Vice-Chairman of the Younghusband Committee and subsequently a member of both the Seebohm Committee and a small pressure group which lobbied for such an enquiry (see p. 23).

a universal art, whether it was directed towards children or old people, was it sensible to maintain the structural barriers then in operation? The Younghusband Committee acknowledged that its recommendations could only apply to some social workers but decided to step beyond the limits of their terms of reference in saying

> We should like it to be clear that we fully recognise the importance of social workers in other services. We are also aware that many of the principles on which our recommendations are based, though applied to the social workers within our terms of reference, are of general application [24].

Co-ordination or Reorganization

Not long after the post-war structure of the welfare services came into operation its disadvantages became obvious and appeals began for improved co-operation between the local departments and their staff. In 1950 a joint circular was issued by the Ministry of Health, the Ministry of Education and the Home Office requesting local authorities to consider ways of co-ordinating their services [25]. The circular proposed that a 'co-ordinating officer' be appointed in each authority whose responsibility would be to investigate cases of neglected children and arrange interdepartmental meetings to decide on future treatment. The main focus of concern at that time was the neglect of children within their own homes. Considering the same problem in 1954, Donnison stressed the need to involve the whole family, when individual members of that family came in contact with social work agencies [26]. 'Some families', he argued, 'cannot be fitted for a normal life in the community by grants of material aid or by the work of services that are each concerned only with one aspect of their troubles.' He maintained that an effective 'comprehensive personal service' required that one social worker took primary responsibility for one family, with specialist help if necessary, and that case conferences should be held to allocate a worker to each family in need. This solution, he felt, was preferable to new legislation. By the mid-fifties, however, it appeared that formal co-ordination was having little success. In 1956 a second circular was sent, a circular to local authorities requesting information on the co-ordinating machinery they had developed, only to find that less than 10% had established co-ordinating arrangements [27].

Throughout the following three years the problems of co-ordinating the welfare services were considered by several official groups. The

Herbert Commission on London Government made its criticisms of the arrangements in no uncertain terms.

> The number of agencies who can be concerned in some way with a family in difficulties is legion, and while it is not for us to touch upon the intricate structure of the social services we are concerned that the work should be made as simple and direct as possible for the field workers, so that they can get on with the job and not spend their time form filling and going through various chains of command to get an answer to a simple enquiry. We are also concerned that the arrangements for providing the services should be acceptable to the public, which means that they must be so co-ordinated that the public do not have to spend their time going from one department or place to another in search of help. Our impression was that in many places the services were working reasonably well at ground level because the field workers were making personal contacts with one another but that in some counties this was in spite of the scheme of organisation rather than because of it [28].

Given such disquiet it is perhaps surprising that improved co-ordination was advocated as a solution to the administrative problems of the welfare services for so long. Two further documents published at the end of the fifties, the Ingleby Report on Children and Young Persons and the Younghusband Report on Social Workers in the Health and Welfare Services, maintained that improved co-ordination rather than structural change would increase the effectiveness of the services under their scrutiny. The Younghusband Committee argued for the streamlining of co-ordinating machinery with greater certainty than Ingleby. The former felt that two of the problems being stressed at that time, 'multiplicity of visiting' and 'overlapping of effort', were exaggerated. Indeed it saw some merits in the multiple visiting of problem families, arguing that the more complex a family's requirements, the greater the number of different skills needed for their treatment. It was essential, however, to avoid independent and unco-ordinated visiting by workers who had no agreed approach [29].

Meanwhile the Ingleby Committee was advocating the improvement of co-ordinating arrangements with some caution. Its report argued that structural divisions had brought about 'inter-service rivalries' which militated against smooth co-operation between the staff of different departments. 'There is a tendency', the report maintained, 'for those who first make contact with a family at risk not to call for further help, or to defer doing so with consequent delay in bringing the co-ordinating machinery into operation' [30].

A Family Service?

The Ingleby Committee's conclusion that the problems of the social welfare services should be met through improved co-ordination rather than by structural change was reached somewhat uneasily. Its unease sprang in part from the conflicting evidence it received, for several of the groups presenting their views to the committee felt that structural change was vital and argued for a family service. Amongst these groups were the London County Council's Children's Committee,[1] the Council for Children's Welfare,[2] the Fisher Group[3] and some members of the Fabian Society.[4] Their proposals differed in detail but essentially their argument was that effective social work within families, especially that relating to children and the prevention of juvenile crime, could only be achieved by enlarging the functions of the existing children's departments and giving by them prime responsibility for the care of families with children. The new family department would work in close co-operation with the health, education, welfare and housing departments plus the youth employment service, child guidance clinics, probation officers, almoners and the National Assistance Board.[5] The Ingleby Committee recognized the importance of these ideas but baulked at the problems of implementing them, maintaining,

> It may be that the long-term solution will be in a reorganisation of the various services concerned with the family and their combination into a unified family service, although there would be obvious and formidable difficulties either in bringing all their diverse and often specialised functions into one organisation or in taking away from the existing services those of their functions relating to family troubles in order to secure unified administration of those functions. Any such reorganisation at local authority level might well involve a corresponding

[1] Baroness Serota was Chairman of the committee from 1958 to 1965 and Peggy Jay was a member.

[2] Members of this group included Professor J. Tizard, Dr J. Grad, Dr Simon Yudkin, Peggy Jay, Alma Birk and Margaret Wynn.

[3] Members of the Fisher Group included Mrs G. Fisher, Dame Eileen Younghusband, John Bowlby, Hilary Halpin, C. H. Rolph and Arthur Skeffington.

[4] Members of the Fabian Group included Mary Stewart, D. V. Donnison, Hilary Halpin, Peggy Jay, James MacColl and Peter Townsend. Their views were discussed in Donnison, D. and Stewart, M., *The Child & the Social Services*, Fabian Society, 1958.

[5] See the Fisher Group, *Families with problems—a new approach*, 1958. This pamphlet was based on the evidence of the Fisher Group and the Council for Children's Welfare to the Ingleby Committee.

reorganisation of the functions of the different government departments concerned. These are matters well outside our terms of reference but we urge the importance of their further study by the government and by the local interests concerned [31].

The family service ideas were developed during the early sixties. In 1962, David Donnison argued that such a service should be provided in each area but, unlike most other proponents of a family department, he felt that it could be formed around *either* the children's *or* the health and welfare departments. He foresaw the possibility of integrating this family welfare service with those for the aged, the physically handicapped and the mentally disordered [32]. A pamphlet produced in 1965 by the Council for Children's Welfare suggested that a family department should be set up in two phases, the first phase being to establish the services for children and the second to include those for the elderly [34].

The same year a Fabian publication envisaged such a new department being composed of the existing children's service, domiciliary and environmental services for the under fives, care of the unmarried mother and her child and provisions for homeless families [34]. The premise from which all these proposals began was that an effective family service could only be achieved by giving greater powers and a wider range of services to one local authority department. Moreover, the fact that most of these plans centred around the needs of children and were based on reorganization of the existing children's department was of great significance in later discussions.

Discussion

No one factor explains the demand for a reappraisal of the welfare services in the mid-sixties. The issues which arose were created in part by the post-war decisions on the structure of the welfare services, in part by the demands of an embryonic social work profession and in part by changes in attitudes regarding the nature of social needs. These changing attitudes resulted in the family and the community becoming the foci for social work activity, the institution no longer being acceptable as the universal solution for those unable to remain independent.

Increasing costs put greater emphasis on the need to improve efficiency, and yet there was no machinery for the co-ordinated planning of these services. Such planning was all the more important since it was a period of considerable confusion for those working within these services. Social workers were searching for a professional identity.

Relationships between the staff in different local departments were often strained and the professional organizations, such as they were, found it difficult to agree. Little was known about the welfare services —there are surprisingly few statistics available on the numbers of staff employed and their patterns of work, especially in the earlier years.

The forces for change can be identified fairly easily but it is more difficult to assess their relative weight with any accuracy. There was little agreement amongst those to whom I spoke about which were the most important features. Those who had been associated with the Ministry of Health and the welfare departments tended to stress the issues of community care, specialization and training since these were the ones emphasized by the Ministry and its committees of enquiry. Those closer to the Home Office stressed instead the development of suggestions for a family service, the importance of increasing crime rates and the general accent on prevention. Of course this oversimplifies their position but it seems that the barriers created in 1948 led to two very separate services with few links at the central level. There was some common ground and the issues were not specific to one department or the other but individuals involved in the development of these services since 1948 have very different perceptions of the important events during these years.

2 The Call for an Enquiry

The Family Service Gains Support

In preparing for a general election political parties must try to predict which issues will catch the imagination of the electorate. Although it is not an easy task they can be fairly sure that the issue of rising crime rates will usually loom large. Assuming that this would be so for the election of Autumn 1964, the Labour Party's Home Policy committee appointed a specialist advisory body to consider the issue. A study group under the chairmanship of Lord Longford was formed in December 1963 'to advise the Labour Party on the recent increase in recorded crime and the present treatment of offenders' [1]. Of great importance at this point was the fact that several of those who had argued for a family service in the past were influential members of the Labour Party. They saw their chance to introduce the idea to political circles and used their influence to persuade the party's executive to consider not only the penal aspects of crime but also the role that social services could play in prevention. The result was that the Longford Committee's remit included the consideration of 'new measures, penal and social, required both to assist in the prevention of crime and to improve and modernise our penal practices'.

The report's conclusions were significant because they formed a basis for policy planning within the penal and social work services once the Labour Party came to office. Seven members of the committee took influential posts in the Labour administration and could therefore ensure that the proposals were not forgotten.[1]

Although the committee's primary focus was upon the problem of

[1] Lord Longford became Lord Privy Seal (October 1964); Lord Gardiner became Lord Chancellor (October 1964); Miss A. Bacon became Minister of State at the Home Office (October 1964); Mr A. Greenwood became Minister at the Colonial Office (October 1964); Miss M. Herbison became Minister for Social Security at the National Assistance Board (August 1964); Baroness

increasing crime, and especially juvenile crime, it nevertheless took the opportunity to press for a general overhaul of the social services. 'The administrative structure of the social services', the report argued, 'is ripe for review so that they may grow and develop coherently to meet the needs of an increasingly complex society. Such a review should be undertaken by a high-powered committee, untrammelled by departmental loyalties and interests. It would inevitably take some time. Meanwhile urgent action is needed to remedy the most glaring deficiencies of the present system' [2]. It suggested that a system of family courts should be established for the treatment of young offenders [3]. These would be properly constituted courts of law but the emphasis and atmosphere of the court would be 'essentially human' with the welfare of the family as a whole the primary consideration. However, the Longford Committee saw preventative measures as even more important and argued, as had others before them, that the first step should be the establishment of a new family service: 'This will incorporate and develop some of the functions of existing central and local government departments relating to children and families including the present children's department and parts of the health, welfare and education departments' [4].

Whilst Lord Longford's group were sitting, an official committee considering similar problems in Scotland were reaching the end of their deliberations. In 1961 the Kilbrandon Committee [5] had been appointed 'to consider the provisions of the law in Scotland relating to the treatment of juvenile delinquents and juveniles in need of care or protection or beyond parental control and in particular . . . the procedure of the courts . . .' Its brief was similar to the first part of the Ingleby Committee's terms of reference. Consideration of the prevention of child neglect by local authorities was remitted to a committee of the Scottish Advisory Council on Child Care, [6] but the Kilbrandon Report nevertheless devoted some time to a discussion of care rather than control. Kilbrandon's argument was in some respects similar to that of the Longford group. Children appearing before the courts showed a basic similarity of underlying circumstances. They had 'a common need for special measures of education and training, the normal upbringing processes for whatever reasons having failed or fallen short' [7]. The report recommended that a system of panels

---

Serota became Minister of State at the Department of Health and Social Security (December 1969); Mr J. MacColl became Private Secretary at the Ministry of Housing and Local Government (October 1964).

consisting of lay persons should replace the juvenile courts and that a 'matching field organisation' should be developed. It is interesting that the Kilbrandon Committee's analysis of the problem stressed the deficiencies of the education system much more than did the Longford Group, hence its conclusion that a Social Education Department should be established.[1] Kilbrandon commented that a wider reappraisal of the social services had been prevented by the narrowly defined terms of reference, and that while its proposals had, as a result, been 'directed to a minority of the child population, there was no doubt about the need for further development of the existing services offering advice and guidance to adults in personal and other difficulties' [8].

By October 1964, when Labour was returned to power, there were two major reports, advocating very similar changes, awaiting the reactions of the incoming ministers. Both documents suggested the formation of new structures for the treatment of young offenders and the reorganization of the local authority and social work services so that one department took primary responsibility for the welfare of the family. The immediate reaction of Miss Alice Bacon, who became Minister of State at the Home Office, was to begin planning a policy for young offenders based on the advice of the Longford Committee (of which she had been a member). As an Under Secretary at the Scottish Office, Mrs Judith Hart began working on the proposals of the Kilbrandon Report and a third minister, Douglas Houghton, who made his debut in the newly created role of co-ordinator of the social services, started to develop his own ideas on a family service. As soon as Alice Bacon arrived at the Home Office she made it quite clear that she wished to produce with great speed a white paper outlining future policy for young offenders. Lord Longford, by this time Lord Privy Seal, and others who had been on his committee, were pressing for government action. Miss Bacon had herself been convinced by the logic of the committee's conclusions and saw an opportunity to implement reforms with little opposition or delay. Her civil servants, however, were less convinced that the proposals would be uncontentious. Nonetheless, since the passing of the Children and Young Persons Act, 1963, which gave local children's departments greater power to undertake preventative work with families in need,[2] several of them had been anxious to develop those powers in conjunction with changes in the treatment of young offenders. Following rapid consulta-

---

[1] This was partly because in Scotland the local departments in other fields were small and weak.

[2] Including financial assistance.

tions, the first draft of a white paper was ready for consideration in Cabinet by the Spring of 1965.

Douglas Houghton held two posts within the Labour administration. In addition to his role as co-ordinator of the social services he was the Chancellor of the Duchy of Lancaster. He was a senior minister in the Cabinet and chairman of a number of Cabinet committees, including those on Home Policy and Social Services.[1] As co-ordinator his task was to effect coherent planning between the principal ministers responsible for the social services but he has subsequently maintained that the position was an untenable one. He had no department and therefore only a very small staff and no Treasury vote, yet he was expected to hold a balance between the often conflicting interests of powerful ministers and departments. Given this difficult position, there were few policy proposals Houghton felt able to consider but he thought that one area of policy was pre-eminently suitable for the co-ordinator to develop; a family service, which spanned the remit of several departments. As chairman of the Cabinet committee on the social services he floated the possibility of developing this idea and it was accepted. With his small staff he produced a skeletal plan which he discussed at some length with Miss Bacon and with organizations such as the Association of Municipal Corporations and the County Councils' Association. He also visited Scotland to discuss reactions to the Kilbrandon Report and possible policy developments there but, overall, Houghton's consultations were fairly limited and the proposals produced somewhat embryonic.

The Call for an Enquiry

Planning within the Home Office and by Douglas Houghton did not go unnoticed. By the end of 1964 a number of prominent academics and practitioners within the social services, some closely connected with the Labour Party, became alarmed at the shape the proposals were taking. Some of them, therefore, decided to form a working group to consider the case against a family service. Their concerns were distilled and articulated by Professor Richard Titmuss in a speech he gave in Eastbourne at the Royal Society of Health Conference in April 1965.

It is fashionable at the present time to argue the case for Family Service Departments. As I understand it, the core of this new Department

[1] Other committees he chaired included those on Transport, Farm Prices, the Ombudsman, the Post Office and Economic Development.

would be the Children's Department to which would be transferred certain other responsibilities at present carried in many areas by welfare departments. I must say, I am not happy about this proposal, and for the following reasons. In the first place, it is too family-centred and child-centred . . . We have to remember that a large number of needs arising in the community are not essentially 'family needs'; mentally ill migrants, elderly widows and widowers, the isolates and childless, unmarried mothers and other categories of people who, in an increasingly mobile society might well hesitate before turning to a 'Family Department' . . . Secondly, I suggest that the conception of a Family Service Department is not broad enough. Important welfare responsibilities both residential and domiciliary might remain well outside the province of a Family Service Department (F.S.D.) . . . Thirdly, I am doubtful whether a F.S.D. would effectively bring together within one administrative structure all social workers in the employ of a single local authority.

He called for Departments of Social Service organized on the criteria of services provided rather than on 'categories of clients or particular fragments of need' [9].

The group, which began meeting after the Eastbourne conference, was composed entirely of distinguished individuals interested in the social services who were concerned to ensure that any reorganization of those services was not narrowly conceived.[1] They saw a family service on the lines then indicated as excluding important health and welfare services and possibly pre-empting wider reforms for many years. By late May 1965, the group had produced a memorandum pointing out

[1] The membership was as follows:

* G. M. Aves: former Principal Welfare Officer at the Ministry of Health and a governor of the National Institute for Social Work Training

* D. Jones: Chairman of the Standing Conference of Organizations of Social Workers

*† R. Huws Jones: Principal, National Institute for Social Work Training

† J. N. Morris: Professor of Social Medicine, University of London

‡ T. Raison: Editor, 'New Society'

* B. N. Rodgers: Reader in Social Administration, University of Manchester

* M. Taylor: Director of the London Boroughs' Training Committee and formerly Chief Inspector, Children's Department (L.C.C.)

R. M. Titmuss: Professor of Social Administration, London School of Economics

* L. E. Waddilove: Director, Joseph Rowntree Memorial Trust, York

* Members of staff or Governors of the National Institute for Social Work Training.

† Later members of the Seebohm Committee.

‡ Member of the Plowden Council on Children and their Primary Schools.

that previous committees which considered aspects of the social work services had been precluded by their terms of reference from a comprehensive survey of these services.[1] The memorandum requested an enquiry into the integration of social work services at the local level, the reasons cited for such a proposal reading rather like parts of the Seebohm Report itself. The rationale included the ad hoc expansion of social work since 1948, the overlapping of services, the problem of pin-pointing responsibility for services, the wastage of resources, the difficulty of providing effective preventative services and of improving professional skills.

The group wished to see the enquiry cover all the work of the local authority children's and welfare departments and social work services in the local authority departments of health, education and housing. There was some disagreement over whether the probation service should be included as part of the terms of reference but the majority reluctantly decided that it would be impracticable to do so since, in any case, there was likely to be considerable opposition from the Home Office to an enquiry. Any suggestion that probation should be a part of the reorganization would only exacerbate Home Office hostility. The group achieved agreement by drafting their proposals carefully; the enquiry should be *concerned with* all the work of the local children's and welfare departments, and with social work services in the health, education and housing departments but it should only *take account of* probation and after-care, social work within hospitals, the social security services and relevant voluntary bodies.

The case was concluded as follows:

> Major developments in social work services are taking place and with only incidental consideration of the total position . . . If separate and isolated developments are allowed to continue, the welfare of large numbers of people will be affected adversely especially the welfare of the more socially handicapped and vulnerable members of the community [10].

They envisaged a speedy enquiry. No period was mentioned in their memorandum but the group were talking in terms of twelve months. This was to some extent tactical to avoid criticism that a committee of enquiry would mean delay but it also reflected a somewhat more limited view of what needed to be done than was later found to be the case by the Seebohm Committee.

More important than the memorandum itself was the success with

[1] This is reproduced as Appendix Two.

which individual members of the group attracted the attention of ministers. The document was sent to Douglas Houghton and a copy to each of the principal social service ministers. On receipt of the memorandum Richard Crossman, who was Minister of Housing and Local Government at the time, wrote to Robin Huws Jones saying that he felt it was important and requesting a meeting. It was decided that Richard Titmuss, a personal friend of Crossman's, should discuss the matter with him. Jerry Morris and Robin Huws Jones both had frequent contacts with Kenneth Robinson, the Minister of Health, and took the opportunity on one occasion to discuss their ideas with him. Both ministers gave their general support to the proposals and made their opinions known to Douglas Houghton, who was very surprised and disappointed to discover opposition to his family service ideas and showed some reluctance to modify them.

Alice Bacon too was anxious that this criticism should not delay her white paper, and the issue was raised at Cabinet level. The result was that the Home Office white paper was redrafted to exclude comments on a family service apart from the announcement that 'the form and scope of such a service will need detailed consideration. The government, therefore, propose to appoint a small independent committee to review the organization and responsibilities of the local authority personal social services and consider what changes are desirable to ensure an effective family service' [11]. Douglas Houghton was asked to suspend development of his plans until the results of the independent committee were known.

Why was a committee of enquiry chosen as the planning machinery for this policy? At the Scottish Office Judith Hart decided, in preference to a formal enquiry, to appoint three expert advisers to work with civil servants on plans for Scotland. This process achieved legislative change almost two years ahead of that in England and Wales. Several reasons were given by the minister and civil servants involved in the decisions regarding planning machinery. Mrs Hart felt that in Scotland it was possible to plan without the constraints of departmental rivalries since all the services in question came under the aegis of the Secretary of State for Scotland. In contrast, the structure in England and Wales was such that four ministries shared responsibility for aspects of social work: the Home Office and the Ministry of Health were the two departments administering most of the services but the Ministry of Education and the Ministry of Housing and Local Government also had interests to promote and protect. Any consideration of comprehensive reorganization had to include all four departments, a delicate balancing process which would probably have reached stalemate if internal departmental planning had been attempted without the framework of a committee's conclusions to consider. In the opinion of the civil servants to whom I spoke, at central government level the political sensitivity of the issues involved was such that a committee of enquiry was the only solution. A second reason put forward by some of those involved was that, in England and Wales, deep divisions of opinion existed between professional groups working within the social services field as to the preferred pattern of reorganization. In Scotland, however, such groups were less well developed, enabling Judith Hart and her advisers to achieve a compromise through informal departmental consultations rather than a committee. The Cabinet decision to establish a committee of enquiry for England and Wales appears to have been based on the belief, first, that it was impossible to achieve interdepartmental planning without an independent committee and, second, that a period of education both for the professionals involved and the public was essential before reorganization could be achieved.

The Committee is Formed

The Committee on Local Authority and Allied Personal Social Services took six months to establish. Some civil servants have suggested that this was an abnormally lengthy period and, if they are correct, it reflects the difficulties of reconciling a number of competing interests in the delicate process of determining the *membership* and *terms of reference* of an interdepartmental committee. Since these factors probably have a greater influence on committees than the evidence they receive, negotiations at this stage are bound to affect departmental fortunes in the future. From July to December 1965, a series of meetings took place between the four departments concerned and Douglas Houghton. As co-ordinator Houghton had no powers to establish a committee. It was partly this lack of executive power which, in effect, reduced the role of the co-ordinator to little more than a figurehead. Instead, the Home Secretary, Sir Frank Soskice, as the senior minister involved, was asked to appoint the committee in consultation with the other ministers. The Home Office was thus in a strong position to exert its influence. Alice Bacon and her civil servants saw no necessity for an enquiry. At the very least, the committee would delay Home Office planning on young offenders and a family service; at worst, it could recommend a reorganization which would alter the focus of the local authority social work services and perhaps place responsibility for them in the Ministry of Health or some new departments. They were, therefore, anxious to ensure that its composition, its brief and its mode of working minimized the disruptive effect on their department's planning.

Decisions on the *chairman* and *terms of reference* were taken before any consideration of the membership. Opinions differ as to just how obvious was the choice of Sir Frederic (now Lord) Seebohm as chairman. Some of those I asked maintained that there were other equally likely candidates for the post but most have taken the view that it was, at the time, a fairly predictable decision. His family background combined successful commercial and banking interests with a well-known concern for social problems (Seebohm Rowntree was a distant cousin). Amongst his many banking interests Frederic Seebohm had been a director of Barclays Bank Ltd. since 1947 and became chairman of Barclays Bank D.C.O. in 1965. Evidence of his philanthropic concern was his long-standing association with the Family Service Units and the National Council of Social Service (he was treasurer of the Sheffield Council of Social Service before the war). He was, in addition, chairman of the York Community Council and the National Institute for Social Work Training, and a trustee of the Joseph Rowntree Memorial Trust.

In October 1965, Seebohm was asked to chair the committee and he agreed to do so on the understanding that certain changes were made. He requested that one name be added to the membership list and asked for modifications to the terms of reference. It was agreed that one further member would be appointed in order to add weight to the social worker interests on the committee. One of Seebohm's objections to the terms of reference was the inclusion of the by now emotive phrase 'a family service'. The term was included even though the most important reason for establishing the enquiry was to examine alternatives to the family service proposals already in existence. After discussion, the brief was modified, but only marginally and the family service reference remained. The final wording was as follows: 'to review the organisation and responsibilities of the local authority personal social services in England and Wales and to consider what changes are desirable to secure an effective family service' [12]. The framing of these terms of reference reflects a general concern by all the social service ministers to protect their existing responsibilities, but in particular it bears the mark of Home Office efforts to limit the purview of the committee.

Frederic Seebohm was not able to persuade the Home Secretary to remove the term 'family service' but he made it quite clear that he did not intend to be restricted by it and indeed the definition used in the committee's report indicates how widely the phrase was interpreted. 'We decided very early in our discussions,' the committee argued, 'that it would be impossible to restrict our work solely to the needs of two or even three generation families. We could only make sense of our task by considering also childless couples and individuals without any close relatives: in other words everybody' [13]. Seebohm underlined his determination to avoid association with the Home Office plans by objecting to the proposal that his committee should be termed 'the Family Service Committee', preferring the more comprehensive but cumbersome title later adopted. It is ironic, however, that despite the chairman's aversion to this title, all the committee's documents were referred to, and indexed as, Family Service Committee Papers.

A second aspect of the brief which caused difficulty was whether the committee could consider the allocation of responsibilities amongst central government departments. Frederic Seebohm wished his committee to consider this because he saw many of the existing problems resulting from divided central responsibility, but he was instructed that the enquiry could not make recommendations on the organization above local authority level.

Thirdly, decisions had to be taken on the range of services to be considered. The focus of the committee was to be the organization of those services which could ensure more effective support for families in need of help but this did not cover the local operations of services such as the National Assistance Board, the voluntary organizations and, most important, the probation service. The issue of whether probation should be included was delicate. The working group which contributed so much to the establishment of the enquiry did not feel that it was wise to suggest that the probation service should become a central part of the committee's brief because of the extent to which this would have affected Home Office planning. If proponents of an enquiry had pursued the argument that, in addition to delaying the planning of a family service, the committee should also hold up a policy on young offenders, their whole campaign might well have failed. Seebohm was reluctant to exclude probation but realized that the Home Office was adamant on this issue. The latter maintained that, as the probation service was in part centrally administered, it automatically remained outside the brief of a committee which was concerned with local services. Increasingly the probation officer's role was being extended beyond the supervision of young offenders to include the after-care of released prisoners. This strengthened the links with the centrally organized prison service. This trend was officially recognized when, on 1 October 1964, a new Probation and After-Care Department was established at the Home Office. Thus, paradoxically, the part of the social services which had been used as a catalyst for reform, juvenile crime, was excluded from the debate on reorganization at this point. Planning for young offenders continued within the Home Office in complete isolation from that for the local authority social work services.[1] The terms of reference were finally clarified by the Home Secretary and accepted by Seebohm in late November 1965.

Membership of the committee

Choosing the members of the committee was as contentious as framing its terms of reference. Again, departmental rivalry played an important part in that, although the members sat as individuals and not as representatives of any particular sectional viewpoint, the ministers involved were anxious to see that their interests were sympathetically recognized, if only informally. A series of meetings, chaired by the Home Secretary, was arranged between the ministers and civil servants of the departments concerned and a number of members were chosen. The final list comprised those not actively opposed by any one ministry which may explain why a number of prominent names from the social services field were omitted. The committee was composed of a group whose views and allegiances were fairly well known to those conversant with the key academics and practitioners within the social services. Their backgrounds and any published work available at the time suggest that two members could be associated closely with the interests of local government, two with those of the Home Office and children's services, two less closely identified with the Home Office, two having close contacts with the Ministry of Health and one with more tenuous links but still broadly concerned with the health and welfare services. In terms of probable departmental affiliations therefore the committee was fairly balanced.

Of course the official rationale for the choice of members was rather different. There were, it was argued, to be three 'representatives'[2]

[1] This separate policy development produced the Home Office white paper, *Children in Trouble*, H.M.S.O., April 1968, Cmnd. 3601, and the Children and Young Persons Act, 1969. See p. 67.

[2] Although the members were described as 'representatives' they sat as *individuals* rather than as formal representatives of particular interests.

from the local government world—one from a county, one from a county borough and one from London. They were Sir Charles Barratt, the Town Clerk of Coventry, W. E. Lane, the Clerk of Lindsey County Council and Baroness Serota, formerly Chairman of the London County Council Children's Committee, Deputy Chairman of the Inner London Education Authority, a member of the Longford Committee, the Royal Commission on the Penal System, the Latey Committee on the Age of Majority and the Central Advisory and Training Councils on Child Care. Both Sir Charles Barratt and Mr Lane had been closely involved with the Local Authority Associations as advisers; the former to the Association of Municipal Corporations and the latter to the County Councils' Association.

Four 'representatives' were to be drawn from the academic world—a doctor, a lecturer in social administration, a lecturer in social work and an expert in the training of social workers. They were respectively, Professor J. N. Morris, Professor of Social Medicine at London University, Director of the Medical Research Council's Social Research Unit and a member of the Royal Commission on the Penal System; Dr R. A. Parker, Lecturer in Social Administration at the London School of Economics and a former social worker with research interests in the fields of child care and housing; P. Leonard, Lecturer in Social Work at Liverpool University and with social work experience in Family Service Units, as a Child Care Officer and Psychiatric Social Worker; R. Huws Jones, Principal of the National Institute for Social Work Training, formerly Vice-Chairman of the Younghusband Committee on social workers in health and welfare services and a member of the Williams Committee on the staffing of residential accommodation. One member was included for his experience with voluntary organizations—M. R. F. Simson, Secretary of the National Corporation for the Care of Old People. Lady James of Rusholme was selected for her interests in the field of education and voluntary work, as a magistrate, as a manager of an approved school and to provide the committee with a second woman.

The choice of membership was criticized on three main grounds. Social workers emphasized the lack of field-level workers and representatives of the social work organizations. The editor of *Case Conference* Kay McDougall, commented: 'To say that many social workers are very perturbed about the make-up of the committee would be putting it mildly. We are told from various sources that the aim has been to appoint a truly independent committee and not a collection of vested interests but there is much to be said for clearly identifiable vested interests for at least they can be allowed for' [14]. In view of the committee's composition she urged social workers to organize their ideas clearly in order to influence the committee with evidence if not through the membership. The comment was valid in that the only local authority members were town clerks rather than chief officers or field-workers and the rest of the committee were largely academics rather than members of professional bodies. Civil servants involved in the choice of members have argued that a genuine attempt was made to construct a committee which would reach a conclusion. To have bowed to the social workers' wishes would have been to risk a report too divided to be useful as a basis for policy planning. The views of social workers may not have been ignored completely. Rumours as to the possible membership of the committee reached a number of those politically active in social work circles and pressure was brought to bear on the Home Secretary to modify the proposed group to include more individuals sympathetic to the social work cause. It is possible that the representations made to the Home Secretary influenced his decision to accept Seebohm's request for an additional social worker on the committee.

In contrast to this view, a second criticism was that, from the interests of the members, it could be predicted that undue emphasis would be placed on the development of a social work profession to the detriment of the clients. In a later examination of the choice of members, Adrian Sinfield wrote that:

> the public and private reaction of the vested interests to the Seebohm Report cannot but heighten anxiety that a major function of the Report has been to strengthen the position of the [social work] profession and of its administrators. The Committee itself consisted essentially of the various vested interests, particularly from the National Institute for Social Work Training, the Staff College of the Social Work profession [15].

The involvement of the National Institute for Social Work Training was certainly considerable. Frederic Seebohm was its chairman, Robin Huws Jones was its principal and Lady James' husband was its president. Peter Leonard later became a senior member of its staff but had only informal contacts there when he was appointed.

The third major criticism came from the medical lobby which, perhaps not without justification, pointed to the imbalance of medical and social work representation. Professor Morris was the only member with medical expertise and was, moreover, known to be critical of the standards of the existing health departments. However, despite what might now appear to be very good grounds for being sceptical about the representative nature of the committee, none of the medical associations made any public criticism of the membership until after the report was published. This slow reaction is perhaps partly explained by the medical profession's refusal to take the committee seriously in the early stages. It was only later when some of their preserves appeared to be in danger that they began to react. Their slow response to the question of membership is characteristic of the role of the medical lobby throughout the campaign for reorganization; they were continually too weak, too divided and too late to be effective. This contrasts markedly with the efforts of a few social work lobbyists, in particular some members of the Association of Child Care Officers, to influence the committee even in the early stages of selecting the membership.

In September 1968, *Public Health*, the official journal of the Society of Medical Officers of Health, carried a special report on the committee. Part of it was devoted to the selection of members.

> During the two and a half years of the Seebohm Committee's life there have been a great many forecasts of its findings. These have been so confident and so consistent as to lead a considerable number of people, to the belief that the committee might, in a sense, be working to a brief, but it is *prima facie* distinctly improbable that ten people of integrity would have consented to serve on the committee if there were to be any external direction of its findings. On looking at the membership, however, one cannot avoid the conclusion that the ten people would inevitably have been likely to reach conclusions on certain lines. The 'heavy artillery' among the ten are people primarily interested in, experienced in and identified with the social sciences . . . There is only one medical member, Professor J. N. Morris . . . Professor Morris ought . . . to have had the company of an MOH or GP; he did not. It is hardly surprising that doctors in general and public health doctors in particular should feel that they have been judged—and in some degree condemned—by an imbalanced judge and jury [16].

The *British Medical Journal* made its criticism in August 1968.

> As might be expected, the report largely reflects the experience of the committee's members. The only member of the medical profession on it was a distinguished professor of social medicine and it is no disrespect to him to say that the absence from the committee of at least one medical officer of health and one family doctor is remarkable in view of its terms of reference [17].

Discussion

In considering the origins of the Seebohm Committee several wider issues emerge. The most general of these is the vastly complex relationship between social issues and policy change. Unlike the education service and the National Health Service, the social work services cater for minority groups and groups, moreover, with little economic and political power. These services have tended to receive scant government attention because pressures for change are less powerful than demands in other fields. In contrast the levels of adult and juvenile crime are seen by policy-makers as sensitive political issues [18] which have the potential to arouse public feeling and which are, therefore, especially important during election periods. For those interested in achieving more fundamental changes than those just concerning delinquency, the issue of juvenile crime is useful as a springboard. By arguing that the prevention of juvenile delinquency is preferable to cure and that the former can only be achieved by a widespread improvement in social services, it is possible to construct a case for more general reforms. In the policy developments of both England and Wales, and Scotland, those interested in promoting a family service used the issue of juvenile delinquency to further their cause; the Longford and Kilbrandon Reports accepted and developed these ideas, thus offering a useful basis for governmental planning. The former committee put their suggestions in context. 'These proposals', it argued, 'are meant to have a social value far beyond the forestalling of delinquency, important as this is. The Family Service . . . will be concerned with other services positively to promote the health, happiness and well-being of the whole family. . .' [19]. A similar pattern of reform was discernible in the United States. Marris and Rein document in great detail the complex ramifications of Kennedy's Delinquency Programme and the extent to which it formed a base for the Poverty Programme which was itself subsequently a springboard for the Model Cities Programme [20]. Once the solution to delinquency is seen as essentially a strengthening of preventive services wider change becomes possible.

The events presented in this chapter illustrate the need to look below the surface when examining policy change. It is often assumed that, because the appointment of a committee of enquiry was first announced in a Home Office white paper, the decision to establish an enquiry was made by that department. It becomes clear when studying the developments in more depth that the opposite was the case here. The committee was created despite the authors of the white paper rather than because of them, and the announcement was only reluctantly included following Cabinet pressure.

The creation of the Seebohm Committee also illustrates the very powerful constraints placed on concerted planning by the central departmental structure. Until 1965 it had been impossible to achieve an interdepartmental committee of this nature. Indeed, a comparison with the simpler planning machinery used in Scotland, where one department was responsible for all the social work services, underlines the effect of a fragmented administrative structure on policy development in England and Wales. Undoubtedly the difficult gestation period left its mark on the enquiry eventually established. Unable to consider central government reorganization and the probation service, the committee was restricted in two important directions. Any policies put forward could involve only partial reorganization of the social work services, and local restructuring without central reforms would dilute the effectiveness of the solution considerably.

Finally, it is perhaps worth speculating a little on the success of the small interest group which eventually brought about the establishment of an enquiry. Until the spring of 1965 the planning for a family service appears to have progressed, with little hindrance. It seemed a logical extension of the policy furthered by the Children and Young Persons Act, 1963, strengthening social workers' powers to help families in need. Given the momentum which the family service approach had gathered by the early months of 1965, it might seem surprising that the intervention of a few individuals only months before a white paper was due to appear was successful in preventing the policy being implemented. Certainly, the group encountered great opposition, but managed to win its campaign. Some of the ministers and civil servants who received the memorandum analysed its success in the following way. The exercise was well organized and the group rapidly managed to produce a clearly stated case which was strengthened by the apparent unanimity of its members. The scope of discussions about the reorganization of the social work services, which had hitherto centred around the children's department, was skilfully widened, the rationale for a broader reappraisal bringing into play ideas and developments from other parts of these services. Moreover, its case, that vulnerable groups such as the handicapped and the aged would be denied the chance of a more effective service if the plans for a narrower family service went ahead, was difficult to oppose.

Above all, the group was authoritative, with a membership whose collective influence permeated both major political parties, the civil service, the academic world, the medical profession and social work. The very close contacts some members had with the ministers involved meant that the effect of the memorandum could be reinforced by private discussion and together the group could demonstrate that, if necessary, it would be possible to mobilize powerful opposition to the family service.

3 The Seebohm Committee

This chapter is primarily concerned with the 'raw materials' at the committee's disposal—the evidence presented to it and the part played by research findings. Over both of these the committee had some control but, first, we consider three factors which affected the enquiry but over which it had little influence. They all stemmed from decisions taken in Whitehall.

Advisory Group or Committee of Enquiry?

The reason most frequently adduced by policy-makers for the formation of the Seebohm Committee was that an independent enquiry was necessary to avoid the complexities of interdepartmental decision-making. Indeed, the post-war history of planning within the social services bore witness to the difficulties of achieving administrative change through the usual departmental channels. The creation of an enquiry moved the focus of planning for the personal social services away from the civil service but no committee can work in complete isolation from the department or departments which established it. Although the enquiry tried to minimize the influence of its creators by denying them access to the minutes of their proceedings, it was undoubtedly affected by the surrounding political climate. The reservations felt by Alice Bacon and some civil servants at the Home Office towards the committee had been reflected in the framing of the terms of reference.[1]

As the committee began its work, further difficulties arose from differences of opinion within Whitehall as to the function of the enquiry. Some of those involved in developing a family service wished to see the committee operate as a planning or advisory group, producing a quick synthesis of the members' views. In contrast, a larger number, which

[1] See pp. 27–9.

included Richard Crossman, Kenneth Robinson and some civil servants within the Ministry of Health, saw the committee's function as that of monitoring attitudes and changing opinions. Any shift of the local authority departmental boundaries would inevitably involve a change in the balance of power between professional groups, and the committee's role was to collect the views of professionals involved and, of equal importance, to prepare the personnel for the upheaval involved in a restructuring of services.

For the first year the committee was under strong pressure from the former group to report quickly. When they began sitting, Miss Bacon requested that they should publish their conclusions within six months, a time-table which Frederic Seebohm refused to accept. A report produced under these circumstances could have taken no account of the views of interested groups; it would have been merely the collective opinions of the members. Instead, he suggested that a preliminary report should be produced and that a more permanent body should be established to consider the problems in greater detail. This was rejected by Alice Bacon on the grounds that the functions of the long-term group would overlap with those of the ministerial advisory councils already in existence. When the Seebohm Committee had been at work for six months, Miss Bacon again requested that it should complete its report as quickly as possible. Despite forceful criticisms of her white paper, *The Child, the Family and the Young Offender* [1], from magistrates, probation officers and the County Councils' Association in particular, she was determined to draft legislation with only minor modifications to her proposals. The Bill had been allotted a place in the 1967/68 parliamentary session. At this time Seebohm saw June 1967 as the earliest possible completion date for his enquiry but this would have allowed very little time for the Home Office to draft a Bill before the summer recess. It was agreed, therefore, that the final date for the report should be brought forward to May. Subsequently, however, events within the Home Office made it unnecessary to meet this deadline. In December 1965, Roy Jenkins replaced Sir Frank Soskice as Home Secretary. The latter had been content to allow legislation to be planned on the basis of the white paper, despite the obvious disquiet expressed by key interest groups whose co-operation would be crucial to the policy's implementation but the former saw the practical problems involved as more serious.[1] It gradually became clear to Miss Bacon that, at the very least, Jenkins regarded a second

[1] Roy Jenkins' wife was herself a magistrate and this may have influenced his decision.

white paper as necessary before legislation and the time-table was revised accordingly. For the committee this meant a reduction of the pressure to produce a quick report but they had been forced to take many of their important decisions on the method of working, the amount of general information they would collect, and especially whether research would be commissioned, in an atmosphere of uncertainty and pressure.

Servicing the Committee

These early pressures were, in part, responsible for a second difficulty. Most of the members felt that the enquiry was insufficiently serviced. The committee's expenses, secretarial assistance and meeting place were provided by the Ministry of Housing and Local Government, which was chosen for the task as the department least committed to any particular outcome. Equally, however, because of this they had least incentive to service the committee well. Moreover, for much of the time they were preoccupied with the far more important considerations for them of the Royal Commission on Local Government Reform.[1]

Several of the committees operating at roughly the same time as the Seebohm enquiry were allotted one secretary or a secretary and an assistant.[2] The committee on Housing in Greater London [2] fell into this category, while the committee on the Rent Acts [3] and the committee on the Impact of Rates on Households [4] had a secretary and two assistants. In comparison with these, the Seebohm Committee does not appear to have been particularly deprived until the last few months.

Mr P. I. Wolf, a principal at the Ministry of Housing and Local Government, was made secretary to the Seebohm Committee and two assistants were provided for short periods. He was extremely hard-working and provided a very valuable service in organizing and even processing the vast amounts of evidence received by the committee. He produced short summaries of each piece of evidence, a task which saved the members a considerable amount of time. More significantly, it meant that his role within the committee was a crucial one since, to some extent, he must have affected the interpretation of the evidence and the weight placed upon it. In common with many secretaries of

[1] The Royal Commission on Local Government Reform (Maud) was announced in February 1966.
[2] This does not apply to Royal Commissions such as the Royal Commission on Local Government or Advisory Committees such as that of Plowden.

departmental enquiries he played the part of an intelligent layman rather than an expert on the subject matter in question. Without exception the members paid tribute to his valuable contribution throughout most of the committee's proceedings. Unfortunately, however, he was promoted to the Welsh Office early in 1968, leaving the committee without its main secretary during the vital months of draft checking and revision. Consequently, the assistance given to the committee was weak at a crucial period and Seebohm took the opportunity in the foreword to his report to comment on the general problem of servicing committees of enquiry.

> They are today usually composed of people in full-time occupations, examining an important subject which calls for urgent action . . . there is always the risk that unless they are able to work rapidly their report will be overtaken by events. The interval between the appointment of the committee and the publication of the report can also be a period of speculation and considerable disturbance for those whose future may be at stake. I hope therefore that serious study will be given to ways of meeting the burden that members carry, so as to ensure that the reports are produced as quickly as possible [5].

Despite its dissatisfaction with the amount of secretarial assistance it received, the committee was very fortunate in one respect. The Joseph Rowntree Memorial Trust provided a small grant which enabled Roy Parker, a committee member, who was on sabbatical leave from the London School of Economics during 1966–7, to work on the drafting of the report during this period. Without this help the report would almost certainly have taken even longer to produce.

The "Shifting Sands" Problem

Any committee of enquiry considering views of current importance knows that, whilst it is sitting, policy decisions of relevance to its field of interest will be made. The longer it sits, the more acute this problem is likely to become. In the case of the Seebohm Committee, the fact that four departments were involved meant that policy decisions on several fronts were being made during the two and a half years of its existence.[1] The members were aware of the need to keep in touch with these processes and were somewhat critical of the ministries involved for failing to keep them notified of circulars and departmental policy on a number of issues.

[1] See Appendix One.

Whilst the committee deliberated, policy decisions of some importance were being made in all the social service ministries. The Home Office were planning new approaches and redesigning services for young offenders, including the community development projects; the Ministry of Health began an examination of the future of the National Health Service in 1967; the Ministry of Social Security[1] were considering the relationship between social work and cash giving and, in particular, the advantages of implementing a visiting service; the Department of Education were digesting the Plowden Committee proposals for children of primary school age; the Ministry of Housing and Local Government were interested in the deliberations of the Royal Commission on Local Government reform and finally, the Scottish Office had totally replanned social work in Scotland and enacted the reform.

Procedure Within the Committee

The procedure adopted by the chairman was to set aside about four months for general discussion by the committee, during which period it issued requests for evidence to be submitted by the end of April 1966. It is perhaps understandable, given the pressures for a speedy report, that only four months were allowed for the presentation of evidence but unrealistic considering the delegation and consultation procedures some interest groups had to follow. Small amounts of written evidence were still being received during the summer of 1967. By the beginning of May 1966, Seebohm, in consultation with some of the members, had decided that general discussion should give way to more detailed consideration of issues, and sub-groups of the committee were formed. These included groups on children, education and probation, training and manpower, housing and voluntary organizations, organizational problems, community relations, medical issues and, finally, research.

In the language of current decision-making theory the committee's approach to its task was essentially 'incremental' [6]. It started from the problems arising within the existing services, the three main questions to which it addressed itself being as follows. What is wrong with the present local authority personal social services and can improvements be made? If improvements are needed how far are these dependent upon organizational change and changes in the distribution of responsibilities? If there is a case for altering the present organization and

[1] See Appendix One.

distribution of responsibilities, what new pattern should be recommended? A rationalist, as opposed to an incremental, stance would have entailed an attempt to clarify their objectives by defining an effective family service, outlining the pattern of services which could effect those objectives and describing the steps required to reach them. There is no indication that the committee even discussed the possibilities of a rationalist approach.

During the early meetings the members began to define the problems facing them. It is clear that even before any evidence was requested, a partial formulation of the problems had been made. The committee asked for evidence to be submitted under certain headings which were suggested as 'guides' to those wishing to contribute. Under the general heading 'The strength of the case for changes' they suggested subheadings such as 'weaknesses in the present pattern of organisation . . . extent to which these weaknesses might be remedied by greater co-ordination, better training, more resources, other measures not involving radical reorganisation; radical reorganisation' [7]. This formulation of the problem was arrived at early in 1966. Fundamental debates about the essential nature of social work and the concept of an effective family service did not take place until much later. Papers on these topics were circulated within the committee in January and June 1967 respectively [8] but the substance of neither paper appeared in the final report.

Acknowledging that in its request for evidence it might have over-emphasized certain issues, the committee invited groups and individuals to modify the proposed framework if they wished, but nevertheless it perhaps underestimated the power of suggestion. Many of those submitting evidence utilized the suggested headings, especially those who were advocating radical changes. In the final report the underlying causes of weaknesses in the personal social services are classified as lack of resources, inadequate knowledge and divided responsibility [9]. Its formulation is very similar to the early definition which implied that there were problems regarding resources, training and co-ordination. Not surprisingly much of the evidence later confirmed this diagnosis.

Clearly the processing of the evidence was easier as a result of the early classification of material. Given the workload of the committee this was very important. In all, they considered written evidence from 160 organizations and 79 individuals, met representatives from 42 organizations plus 54 individuals, and visited 17 local authorities [10]. It would be wrong to suggest that an ordering of the complexities by careful planning at an early stage is unnecessary but the limitations imposed should be recognized. These will become clearer when considering the issues discussed by the enquiry, but before doing so we examine the committee's 'raw materials'.

The Evidence

As we have seen, a vast amount of evidence varying considerably in quality was presented to the committee; a reflection of the large number of organizations, many of them very small, which represent professional and client groups within the social services. Its volume and content vindicated those who had argued that a committee of enquiry, collecting and analysing the views of interested parties, was an important piece of machinery to include in any consideration of the reshaping of the local authority social services. The deep divisions of opinion exhibited by the main interest groups would probably have been impossible to reconcile by the four ministries involved since they themselves had such differing views. The difficult function of the committee as educator and arbitrator can be demonstrated by examining the diverse views on reorganization presented by the major interest groups.

The most influential documents were of two kinds; there were those which were considered by the enquiry to be distinctive and well argued and presented and those which were received from organizations and groups whose views had to be taken into account by virtue of their status or importance in implementing the eventual policy. Opinions as to the quality of individual pieces of evidence varied, but an example of the former was that of the Islington Social Workers' Group [11] who took the unusual position of arguing cogently for administration of the personal social services by central government. Falling into the second category were, for instance, the four ministries, the British Medical Association and the Association of Municipal Corporations.

It is all too easy in retrospective studies to impose a spurious rationality upon the views and strategies of interest groups and upon the process of evidence presentation. Unfortunately, the number of bodies and variety of views make categorization necessary but it must be remembered that opinion formation and the submission of evidence often take place during a period of considerable confusion. The evidence is discussed here under four headings: the ministries, the social work organizations, the medical and allied organizations and the local authority associations.

The ministries

The Home Office presented several memoranda mostly containing
factual information on the services under its administration, and three of
its senior civil servants gave oral evidence—Sir Charles Cunningham
and Miss S. Clement-Brown in the early stages and Mr Derek Morell
towards the end of the committee's work. In the official view of the
Home Office [12], the crucial question to be answered was whether it
was still necessary to retain a separate local committee and department
to administer services for children in need. The memorandum maintained that the system was ensuring a high standard of care in these
services and that arguments for retaining it had great weight. Nevertheless, the authors accepted that difficulties in co-ordination had
become apparent, accentuated by increased emphasis on the provision
of social work to the child's own family and greater appreciation of the
contribution social caseworkers could make to all social services. Given
these problems it was felt that two solutions merited consideration: a
unitary social casework service bringing together all social workers
employed by a local authority, or a social work department encompassing
the functions which are most directly concerned with family problems
and forestalling family breakdown. After discussion the memorandum
concluded that the objections to the first suggestion were overwhelming,
although the disadvantages do not seem as conclusively damning as the
paper asserts. How, it was asked, could the social worker undertake a
whole range of duties without an inordinately long training or loss of
standards? If one defines 'the family' in a broad sense, however, this
objection applies also to the second solution. Another difficulty put
forward in the Home Office evidence was that if a chief officer from one
of the existing departments was put in charge of the new department,
social workers not belonging to his previous department would have no
clear chain of responsibility. Furthermore, it was argued, this solution
might mean the separation of social casework from other responsibilities
such as residential care or fostering. The outright rejection of this
solution, for the above rather weak reasons, suggests that the Home
Office civil servants had decided to protect the interests of child care
rather than help the committee examine a broader spectrum of social
needs. The discussion of their second suggestion confirms this. They
saw some advantages in the creation of a social work department aimed
at the prevention of family breakdown. However, a major difficulty they
foresaw was that 'there might be a tendency to spread resources more
evenly than at present between, say, the care of children and the care of

the elderly, and this might reduce the resources devoted to child care. The welfare of children in care would become only one of several preoccupations for the new department . . .' Several other minor difficulties were aired but the overall conclusion was that objections to this solution could be overcome if the scope of the department was 'kept within bounds'. They suggested that school attendance enforcement, child guidance, social work with unmarried mothers and mental health social work should remain with the existing departments and that accommodation for the elderly and the home help service should be amongst the last to be considered for a place in the new department. The strategy behind the proposal appears to have been to retain the predominance of child care in any new department by excluding the major competing services and thereby preserve the standard of that service.

The Ministry of Health presented several papers to the committee. Like the Home Office, the Ministry of Health [13] stressed the importance of considering the individual within a social environment but it was quick to point out that any family service should not take as its only criterion for a family the existence of children, important though these were. One-person families, married couples without children and adults with dependants of all ages should also fall within the definition.

The ministry's evidence cited the deficiencies of the system as duplication of function, wasteful use of scarce staff, gaps in services and the difficulties of access. These were, it argued, unlikely to be solved by greater co-ordination alone and they suggested four possible ways of reorganizing the services under review. A social workers' department was put forward but dismissed quickly on the main grounds that social casework would be divided from other types of remedial action and that control of social work in its widest sense would become divided. The solution was not entertained very seriously. An enlarged children's department would, it was maintained, have some merits when considering the welfare of children: there would be a reduction of overlap in function and an increase in effectiveness. As a general solution, however, it was clearly considered unsatisfactory. It would appear that a service designed to meet all the needs of a certain type of client is bound to cut across the pattern of services designed to meet specific needs for all types of client and in this way to lead to duplication and even rivalry [14]. The memorandum cited an example of duplication about which the ministry were particularly sensitive at the time. Some children's departments were beginning to provide home help services although these were administered centrally by the Ministry of Health and were traditionally housed within the local health departments.

The two solutions considered most carefully were, the amalgamation of the health, welfare and children's departments and secondly a new social welfare department. In the former case it was felt that the resulting department would be rather large but it had the advantage of 'simplicity and completeness'. The latter solution had several points in its favour: it would reduce the possibilities of duplication of function and of gaps in services, the wasteful use of scarce skilled staff and the difficulties attaching to services defined by reference to age or other groups. It could provide a single point of reference for the public and would encourage the growth of social work as a single profession and the integration of training for it.

The memorandum did not come down specifically in favour of any one solution, preferring to leave the committee to make its own interpretations. One explanation given to the committee on several occasions was that senior civil servants within the ministry saw the role of government departments *vis-à-vis* committees of enquiry as informative but impartial. This may be the case, but the Home Office officials seemed to interpret their role differently, preferring to be more specific in their suggestions. It is much more likely that there was difficulty within the ministry in reconciling its medical and social work interests and that, as a result, the issues were left open.

It is noticeable, however, that the presentation of the last solution stresses the benefits to social work rather than the difficulties for the Ministry of Health. The memorandum acknowledged that local health departments would be somewhat weakened by the loss of responsibilities which the creation of a social welfare department would involve, and emphasis was placed on preserving for the medical officer responsibility concerning the mentally ill and subnormal. Nevertheless it is surprising that the Ministry of Health, which contained a far larger group of civil servants administering the medical services than those concerned with social work, should minimize the problems that a new social welfare department would present for the Ministry of Health.

The Department of Education and Science presented only factual evidence initially but was later asked by the committee for supplementary information on possible ways of improving the existing pattern of organization. The reply made the department's position quite clear.

While the Department recognises that there are certainly points where the working of the system could be improved, it does not, with the possible exception of the Education Welfare Service, see the need for any fundamental reorganisation. Basically, the system covers four distinct spheres of activity—Education, the work of the Children's Department, Health and Welfare—and while there are dangers involved in this separation . . ., the Department, from the educational aspect, sees no serious or fundamental weakness which calls for elimination or blurring of the distinction between these main spheres [15].

Although maintaining that structural change was unnecessary, the department nevertheless saw the need for greater co-operation between the four spheres. This could be achieved by closer teamwork between officers of the four departments, the creation of regular co-ordinating machinery, the systematic collation of information on those requiring advice and guidance, better training of officials and improved public relations.

Within the field of education it was felt that several changes should be made. Each school should know precisely where to go for social work help, there was great merit in the medical officer of health taking the role of the principal school medical officer, there should be better links between schools and hospitals or G.P.s (the department did not expand on how this could be achieved), and the different functions of special and approved schools should be defined. The only contentious comment was that the education welfare service might develop into a full counselling service for schools. However, they did not commit themselves on the issue, arguing that consideration of the proposals should await the Plowden Council's deliberations.

The Ministry of Housing and Local Government did not submit any evidence on their opinions concerning reorganization of the personal social services but made available a memorandum sent to the Royal Commission on Local Government. The ministry was too preoccupied with local government reform as a whole to show much interest in reorganization proposals for one small sector.

Summarizing the ministries' views, it can be said that the Home Office was able to leave the committee in no doubt as to their views. It was probably helped in that a contentious issue for those interested in the welfare of children—the future of the probation service—had been omitted from the committee's terms of reference. Civil servants at the Ministry of Health were in a more difficult position. Any reorganization would involve a shift in the balance of power between health and welfare interests. Consequently, it was necessary to present a number of options without clearly stating a preference.

Members of the committee have said that they found the evidence from the ministries predictable but this is hardly surprising. Probably more important as a source of opinion were the close contacts some members had with civil servants. Professor Morris and Mr Huws Jones were members of the Minister of Health's study group established in 1965 to examine long-term problems within the health services; Baroness Serota was a member of the Advisory Council on Child Care and the Central Training Council, and Lady James had close links with the Department of Education and Science.

The social work organizations

Despite attempts to create a common identity amongst social workers, some conflicts of interest still existed by 1966 when the groups were asked to give evidence to the Seebohm Committee. The Standing Conference of Organisations of Social Workers,[1] to which most of the leading professional groups belonged, submitted evidence which revealed that complete unanimity could not be reached, and that on some issues there were important differences of opinion. There was agreement that reorganization was desirable but divergence over which groups should be included, how the reorganization should be effected, the central training arrangements and the extent of specialization desirable in the future.

The organizations representing social workers provided very similar analyses of the basic problems requiring attention but this is not surprising. We have already noted that they received considerable help from the committee in presenting their case, since evidence was asked for under clearly prescribed headings [16]. The committee requested

[1] The organizations considered in this section are:
The Membership of the Standing Conference of Organisations of Social Workers
Association of Child Care Officers
Association of Family Caseworkers
Association of Moral Welfare Workers
Association of Psychiatric Social Workers
Association of Social Workers
Institute of Medical Social Workers
National Association of Probation Officers
Society of Mental Welfare Officers

Other important groups representing social workers:
Association of Children's Officers
Association of Directors of Welfare Services
County Welfare Officers' Society
Conference of Principal Probation Officers

views on the extent to which weaknesses could be remedied by greater co-ordination, better training, more resources or radical reorganization. Somewhat predictably the analysis of existing problems tended to be under such headings as lack of co-ordination, poor training provisions, lack of resources and so on. As for the solution, a social services (sometimes called social work) department was suggested and in most cases it was added that a social worker should be put in charge [17]. Within this broad framework, however, there were four important issues over which the major social work organizations disagreed.

The boundaries of the proposed department varied.[1] All the bodies we are considering wished to see certain functions included; those of the existing children's and welfare departments, and personal welfare services from the housing and education departments. There was agreement on this nucleus of services. The differences of opinion concerned two service areas: the extent to which functions from the health departments should be subsumed and whether probation should be included.

On the former question, the Association of Family Caseworkers wished to see several important functions taken over by the new department. These included the mental health, home help and health visiting services plus the medical and psychiatric social work departments of local hospitals. The Association of Directors of Welfare Services were less specific, wishing to include those parts of the health service with high social but low medical significance. All the groups felt that domiciliary services for the mentally ill, mentally subnormal, the elderly and the physically handicapped should be the responsibility of the new department. The groups included the Association of Psychiatric Social Workers [18] and the Institute of Medical Social Workers [19], both of whom contained many members working in hospitals and health departments. The support of these groups for including the mental health services in the proposed social services department added considerable weight to the social workers' case. There were differences as to whether the health visitor should remain in the health department: the National Association of Probation Officers [20] thought she should, but the Association of Family Caseworkers [21] felt she belonged with the social services.

[1] It is not easy to compare the evidence of all the social work groups on boundaries since some, like A.C.C.O. and A.C.O., suggested changes on the basis of services related to certain groups of those in need (services for the old, etc.) whilst others referred to types of social worker (home helps, probation officers, etc.).

Although the Seebohm Committee was precluded by its terms of reference from considering whether the probation service should join any new department, evidence on this issue was presented. The Association of Child Care Officers [22], the Association of Family Caseworkers, the Association of Psychiatric Social Workers and the County Welfare Officers' Society [23] argued that it should be part of the social service department. The Conference of Principal Probation Officers [24] proposed that their service should remain separate, but the National Association of Probation Officers was divided. A majority thought that the best way of developing work with offenders was to maintain probation and after-care outside the local authorities. They felt it was important that the service be seen as independent. Some members argued that any changes should be towards a centralized national service more closely related to the whole penal field. A minority, many of whom worked in London, wished to integrate the probation service with the local authority personal social services so that there would be no doubt that the probation officer was a social worker.

The Standing Conference of Organisations of Social Workers [25], clearly alarmed by lack of agreement as to exactly which services should be included in a radical reorganization, suggested that there should be a period of experimentation before final conclusions were reached. It maintained that there was not sufficient evidence on which to base decisions. The representatives of the Association of Psychiatric Social Workers, arguably the most powerful of the social work groups, agreed on this policy but there was opposition from other bodies. One problem foreseen was that it might be difficult to abolish a pattern of organization once it had been established, even on an experimental basis. Another, put forward by the Association of Child Care Officers, was that experiments might be used to delay radical reorganization nationally.

The Association of Child Care Officers (A.C.C.O.) and the Association of Children's Officers (A.C.O.) [26] made specific suggestions as to how reorganization should be effected. They both proposed that the change-over should be phased and that in the first phase only functions relating to deprived children should be included. Services for other groups were to be introduced in phases two and three. There was little discussion in either paper as to why change should be introduced in that way and both groups were subsequently critized for what was seen by some as a clumsy attempt to establish the predominance of the children's services or the new department [27]. Why did A.C.C.O. and A.C.O. resort to such tactics? Those I questioned felt that the answer lay in the difficulties these groups experienced in achieving internal agreement over reorganization. Some of the staff working within the children's departments felt that they had a lot to lose from a reorganization which removed the distinctions between social workers. Others, a minority, felt that it was only by creating a common identity within social work that progress could be made. Phasing was the compromise. If it had not been adopted, it is likely that both organizations would have been forced to suggest a limited family service centred around the children's services (similar to that proposed by the Longford Committee) rather than the more comprehensive department finally proposed. It appears, however, that by the time representatives of the associations gave oral evidence they had had second thoughts about phasing but the basic solutions proposed by the groups remained intact.

Although differences existed over the exact boundaries of any new department and the way it should be introduced, these were less fundamental than the problems concerning the central training arrangements. The Standing Conference of Organisations of Social Workers devoted much of its time to this issue and whilst the Seebohm Committee were sitting no unanimity amongst members of the conference was reached. Organizations familiar with the Home Office system, such as the Association of Child Care Officers and the National Association of Probation Officers, argued in favour of some departmental influence over the training of social workers and those closely linked with the Ministry of Health stressed the need for independence.[1] The unresolved differences concerning training were played down whilst the committee were sitting and it was only after the report was published, when reactions from organizations were being sought, that a compromise position was reached.[2] In the evidence from social work organizations there was little discussion of central training arrangements. The sections on training concentrated instead on defining the social worker's role, suggesting modifications to the content of courses and requesting an increase in the number of staff recruited. A fourth preoccupation concerned the range of duties individual workers should ideally perform. Should there be greater specialization within social work and if so, along what lines and at what level? This was no new issue; we have already looked briefly at attempts to create one social work profession.[3] For some, a prerequisite of unification had been a

[1] See pp. 71–2 for a detailed explanation of why these differences of opinion arose.
[2] See p. 89.
[3] See pp. 11–14.

largely generic training which had slowly been introduced since the early fifties.

There were groups, however, which accepted some common content to all social work courses but argued strongly that certain specialist elements should be retained. The most vociferous of these was the Association of Psychiatric Social Workers (all the members of which were well qualified). In its evidence it stated:

> Most members of the association, though welcoming a more flexible approach to the treatment of social problems and greater inter-changeability between workers, do not subscribe to the concept of an all-purpose social worker . . . specialisation is essential to the advance of knowledge . . . Furthermore, it is neither possible nor desirable for one person to be familiar with all aspects of legislation and administrative detail in relation to the many problems which affect clients . . . Some people will find work with certain types of clients more within their capacity and also more satisfying than with others [28].

The National Association of Probation Officers' evidence expressed a similar view.

> We think it important [it maintained] to recognise that within this new social service department there will still be a need for specialisation. The association considers that it is important for the public to have a number of different points of access to the personal social services. The way in which clients view their own problem often determines the kind of service to which they go in the first instance . . . we think that it should be possible for a larger social service department to work through local offices and to retain identifiable specialist workers . . . [29].

The Standing Conference members agreed that a variety of social worker roles was necessary. 'Some clients would best be helped from the beginning by a specialist social worker; others would be helped by one social worker meeting various needs, and others would require the help of several social workers.' The organizational implications of this, it felt, were that 'district offices should be large enough to be able to employ some social workers with specialist skills, for example, in work with the mentally disturbed or in marital casework or group work' [30].

Despite disagreement over important aspects of reorganization, partly by accident, partly by design, the social work groups presented a common basic framework. Those who were members of the Standing Conference had had opportunities to reach general conclusions at conference meetings. Those outside the organization recognized the potential gains for the social work profession which the Seebohm

Committee offered; the very real possibility of a single, powerful local authority department from which to practise. Although there were differences in the interests of the groups these were played down in the evidence, thus providing the enquiry with a broad solution to which it could respond; a solution, moreover, which tended to confirm the views of most of its members.

The medical and allied organizations

The main organizations representing general practitioners and medical officers which gave evidence were the British Medical Association (B.M.A.),[1] the College of General Practitioners (C.G.P.),[2] the Society of Medical Officers of Health (S.M.O.H.)[3] and the Association of County Medical Officers (A.C.M.O.).[4] They suggested a variety of solutions to the committee. The B.M.A. and S.M.O.H. maintained that some reorganization was necessary whilst the C.G.P. and the A.C.M.O. argued that improved co-ordination of existing agencies could solve most of the problems of providing an effective service to those in need.

The B.M.A. and the S.M.O.H. stressed the need to strengthen links between the health and welfare services, arguing that certain social services should be combined under the health department, still headed by the medical officer of health. The B.M.A.'s proposed 'health and social services department' was to embrace the existing health, welfare and children's departments in order that the service 'should be capable of dealing with any social or medico-social problem referred to it and not limited to some specific need' [31]. The 'health and welfare department' advocated by the S.M.O.H. differed from the B.M.A.'s mammoth department in that it excluded the children's services. The society felt that co-ordination could be achieved through a 'family services committee' consisting of representative members from the existing committees concerned with social services. Both these groups defined the problem in similar terms to most of the social work organizations. They

[1] The B.M.A. represents both G.P.s and M.O.H.s, although the latter form only a small proportion of the membership. In 1972 approximately 1,700 medical officers working in local authority service belonged to the B.M.A. (3% of its total membership).
[2] Now the Royal College of General Practitioners.
[3] The society has approximately 1,900 members, not all of whom are local authority medical officers. (Some are academics, others are medical officers working within H.M. Forces, etc.)
[4] Most of the association's members are also members of S.M.O.H.

stressed the overlapping of functions, the multiplicity of visiting and divided responsibility. Their solution was unification but, unlike the social worker proposals, the focus was the health department and the medical officer of health was to be in control.

The College of General Practitioners proposed no organizational changes relating to the social services, concentrating instead upon the difficulties caused by the tripartite structure of the health services and the importance of co-ordination between doctors and social workers. Experimentation, it maintained, should take place before action was taken on a national scale to avoid 'a doctrinaire approach unsupported by practical experience' [32]. The A.C.M.O. argued that radical reorganization to produce a large, all-purpose department was unwise. It pointed out that the failure of the Poor Law administration had indicated that welfare needs should be met by specialist departments, and added, 'The development of social work suggests that, even if a department were created it would require so many sections that the "omelette" would immediately divide into the constituent eggs' [33].

Those bodies representing para-medical staffs[1] presented evidence which indicated their wish to remain under medical control. Whereas social workers were at this stage rejecting the idea of being subordinate to the G.P. or the medical officer in a community team, the health visitors, district nurses and midwives still seemed to accept it quite readily. The Health Visitors' Association, in conjunction with the Royal College of Nursing, gave very positive evidence calling for a family health and welfare department similar to that proposed by the B.M.A. It included, in addition to health and welfare services, environmental health, the children's services, the work of educational welfare officers and the child guidance services [34]. When asked where health visitors would wish to work if a unified social services department was established, the association replied that a survey indicated that health visitors were ten to one in favour of remaining with the health department. The Royal College of Midwives had no positive suggestions for reorganization but argued against the creation of a new social work department because it would destroy the existing teams under the medical officer [35]. Similarly, the Queen's Institute of District Nursing stressed the need to retain and develop teams under the leadership of general practitioners. The Association of Public Health Lay Administrators argued that social work should not be confused with the social services since the former affected only a small section of the public and

---

[1] Those bodies representing mental health workers have been included under social work organizations, although they could equally have been included here.

it was unnecessary and confusing to operate the latter, like the former, in a family setting.

In contrast to the evidence from social worker organizations, where a basic similarity in the proposals for reorganization could be found, the medical and para-medical organizations mentioned above wanted a variety of outcomes from the committee. Tactically, the groups adopted two main approaches. The first was to argue that no structural change was necessary; increased co-ordination could prevent the overlapping of services and fill existing gaps. The second was to propose reorganization in various forms with the medical officer in overall command. This lack of unanimity undoubtedly lessened their chances of success. There was no solution open to the committee which could satisfy them all. Why was there no consultation between groups over possible strategies? It appears that at the stage of evidence presentation many of them did not regard the existence of the committee as any great threat to their preserves. Most of the evidence specifically stated that medical control over health and welfare should be retained but no case for this was made out. It was assumed to be generally acceptable. Moreover, the quality of the medical evidence was poor. That little effort had been vested in its preparation was demonstrated when one society even quoted the committee's terms of reference incorrectly as relating to the local authority personal *health* services of England and Wales [36].

The local authority associations

The major local authority organizations which presented evidence to the committee were the Association of Municipal Corporations, the County Councils' Association, the Rural District Councils' Association, the London Boroughs' Association, the Society of Town Clerks, the National Association of Local Government Officers and the Institute of Municipal Treasurers and Accountants. Most of the evidence is muddled and indecisive. In part, this can be explained by the preoccupation in local government circles with the forthcoming Royal Commission on Local Government which had been announced in February 1966. (The bulk of evidence from these groups was presented in the spring and summer of that year.) For two of the most powerful groups, the A.M.C. and C.C.A., it can be explained, in part, by the difficult problems posed for them by the committee's remit. Any reorganization of the personal social services would involve a redistribution of power between local authority departments and therefore between chief officers. Since membership of A.M.C. and C.C.A. included education officers, housing managers, children's officers, welfare officers and medical officers of health, the formulation of evidence was inevitably a delicate process.

On the question of structural reorganization, the County Councils' Association, the Society of Town Clerks and the National Association of Local Government Officers supported radical change, but the County Councils' Association's recommendations were the only ones which were carefully argued. The C.C.A. maintained that county and county borough councils should have a statutory responsibility to establish a social services committee and a department with its own chief officer. These committees would be responsible for the existing duties of welfare departments, children's departments, the social work functions of education departments and health departments and the provision of social work services on an agency basis for housing departments. Thus far the diverse interests of the C.C.A. membership could be reconciled. There were, however, no recommendations on which chief officer should head the new department or which skills were necessary for the job.

The Association of Municipal Corporations did not specify whether it thought radical reorganization was necessary, while, in contrast, the London Boroughs' Association maintained that radical changes would be premature. It argued that the anomalies of the existing system extended beyond the personal social services and, secondly, that the services in Greater London had recently undergone major changes and that further upheavals would severely affect their quality. Improved co-ordination would, it suggested, remove many of the existing difficulties.

When considering the timing of possible changes, the point upon which most of the local authority groups agreed (only a few failed to mention it) was that, whatever conclusions the Seebohm Committee finally reached, no changes should take place until plans for the reform of local government became known. They predicted quite correctly that the committee might press for reorganization of one sector within local government before a policy on the reform of the whole system could be agreed.

The issue of central control over local government was one of major importance to the committee, but, interestingly, the local authority groups clearly did not think that it would be. Had they done so, it is likely that some discussion of local autonomy would have been included in their evidence, especially as it was probably a problem about which most of their memberships would have agreed. After the publication of the committee's report the associations devoted considerable time to the issue—arguing that the report placed too much emphasis on central control over local government.[1]

The evidence from local authority groups and from individual authorities was difficult for the committee to process. Much of it was poorly presented, and recommendations on the pattern of reorganization differed. One of the most problematic issues for the enquiry to consider —the nature of relationships between central and local government in any reorganization—was ignored. The only unequivocal position taken by these associations was the importance of awaiting local government reform before deciding on the future of the personal social services.

Research and Information

The committee decided to commission no original research despite evidence from several groups[2] that some systematic evaluation of services was necessary prior to the formation of final conclusions and despite the comments of several previous committees that new research into aspects of the social work services was required [37]. The reasons for deciding against commissioning new work were not financial ones, since the Joseph Rowntree Memorial Trust had promised the committee funds for such purposes. The understanding was that if the Ministry of Housing refused to reimburse the committee's research expenses the Trust would do so. We have already discussed the fact that when the committee was first established it was under pressure to report quickly. From the outset, therefore, it appeared to the members that there would be little time for the sponsoring of a major research programme. The committee's report, however, justifies their decision on other grounds.

> First, there is the difficulty of setting up and evaluating live experiments in such a major and complex field; second, the time required would only prolong the uncertainty about the future which has followed the setting up of this enquiry. This is damaging morale in the services and discouraging progressive development. Third, we doubt whether such experiments in this particular field would produce clear and reliable results . . . This does not mean that we are opposed to research and experiment: quite the contrary. Ideally it should precede

---

[1] Discussed on p. 49.

[2] See, for example, the evidence from the Standing Conference of Organisations of Social Workers and the College of General Practitioners.

change; practically it becomes possible only when problems are identified and investigated sufficiently early and machinery exists for continuous research to be undertaken. Since these conditions do not prevail in the present personal social services, we believe that organisational changes should so be designed that the changes themselves are evaluated and the sensitive flexibility of the services encouraged [38].

A short research project considered by the committee was provided, at their request, by Dr Bleddyn Davis, who was studying the relationship between local authority needs and resources. Part of this work involved an examination of variations in the standards of provision of health and welfare services. The committee was interested in the more specific question of whether combined health and welfare departments were more or less effective than separate ones but unfortunately the results proved inconclusive [39]. Two other reports were submitted for consideration by the committee. Mr Michael Power and Dr Jean Packman brought together the available information on the number of children suffering from mental, physical and social handicaps of various kinds and compared them with the number of children known to be receiving help. The National Child Development Study (1958 cohort) produced a report drawing evidence from their project relating to children in need of social care [40].

Although the committee failed to generate new research, its own collation of existing evidence provided a useful picture of the local authority personal social services in the mid-sixties. Information was included on variations in patterns of provision and expenditure between local authorities, the committee and administrative arrangements, the staff employed in the services under review, the organization of training and salary scales.

Discussion

Clearly the reasons for establishing an enquiry can affect both the way it works and its reception afterwards. The fact that there was no agreement within Whitehall as to the role of this particular enquiry meant that, for the first few months, the members were somewhat unsure of their time-table. Nevertheless, members were clear in their own minds that their role was both to canvas opinion on desirable changes within the personal social services and to inform those working within the services of the possibilities open to them. Therefore, the committee took the reception of evidence very seriously but controlled its content to some extent by suggesting the format in which it might be presented.

Thus the process of education began very early, the committee functioning both to receive opinion and to mould it.

The presentation of evidence demonstrated a wide variety of opinion between pressure groups within the same profession. It was striking, however, that the social workers managed to achieve a considerable measure of agreement whilst there is no evidence that, at this stage, the other major interest groupings even tried. Nevertheless, although by the mid-sixties social work organizations had demonstrated a willingness to plan together, these organizations seemed professionally unsophisticated in some respects when compared with their medical colleagues. Generic courses had been established in several universities and colleges but there were still two training councils—one responsible for child care training and the other for courses relating to work within the health and welfare services. The differences in professional status can be demonstrated by the contrast in their relationship with ministries regarding policy making. The B.M.A. had long been in constant and close touch with the Ministry of Health concerning a wide range of policy issues affecting the medical profession. For social workers there were no such formal contacts. The Home Office, for instance, refused to negotiate with the Association of Child Care Officers, arguing that the departments' links with the local authority associations covered the interests of child care officers. Given the differences between the two professions, it is remarkable that the social workers emerged from the Seebohm debate more satisfied than the medical officers. In part the explanation lies in forces outside their control but an examination of the strategies of the two groups suggests that social workers took the personal social services much more seriously than the medical profession and mobilized their resources much earlier and more effectively.

4 One Door? The Committee's Decisions

Chapter Three examined the 'raw materials' at the committee's disposal but it told us little about how these materials were used. This chapter looks at the issues the committee decided to tackle and the interplay of members' views, evidence and research upon the final decisions. It has to be remembered that it is often difficult for those involved in making decisions to reconstruct the reasons for choosing one suggestion rather than another. Members may have reached the same decision by different routes. Moreover, the compromises, trade-offs and alliances are often too sensitive to make public. For these reasons, it is only possible here to look fairly broadly at the issues and their resolution.

The first and most important task was to consider the question of structural reorganization of the services under review and it was from this decision that most of the other issues followed. However, it consumed little of the committee's time in comparison with the issues arising from it. The two which predominated were the delineation of the boundaries around the new department and the relationship between central and local government. Others, of lesser weight, included specialization, training, the introduction of reforms, the implications of its proposals for London (which had only recently undergone reorganization itself) and the development of the social work services in Scotland.

It has sometimes been argued that most of the members of the committee had decided that they were in favour of one central department responsible for social work and related activities before they joined the enquiry. It is claimed that, whilst decisions were made within the committee, they were ones which flowed from the basic assumption that there would be a single department. In chapters One and Two we saw that the suggestion for a unified department was not new but that these earlier proposals centred upon the children's department and related mainly to the problems of children. The Seebohm Committee was concerned with a wider range of needs, including those of the handicapped, the mentally ill and subnormal and the elderly. Nevertheless, the principle of unification was one which had received much discussion in social work circles before the enquiry was established and the assumption that improved co-ordination could solve the structural problems had been somewhat discredited. Although, therefore, the committee members may have made every effort not to prejudge the pattern of reorganization, they began their work with the concept of unification well to the fore.

The Pattern of Reorganization

The committee's interpretation of the *problems* which faced it severely limited the *solution* it was likely to choose. In its report, the shortcomings of the personal social services were listed as inadequacies in the amount, range and quality of provision, poor co-ordination, difficult access and insufficient adaptability. It maintained that at the root of these weaknesses lay three main problems—*lack of resources, inadequate knowledge* and *divided responsibility*.

Given this definition of the problem, the 'alternatives' to a unified department which it finally proposed seem unlikely candidates. Since divided responsibility was held to be one of the major sources of the weakness in the services, co-ordination of the existing structures was unlikely to be chosen. Similarly, the solutions which involved creating two major local authority departments responsible for the social work services would involve continuing co-ordination problems between social workers. The committee considered the possibility of suggesting two social services departments, one responsible for social work services for children and families with children and the other for old people and handicapped adults. A variant of this was that the personal social services should be divided between an enlarged children's department and a combined health and welfare department. Both suggestions had the advantage of simplifying the structure somewhat without causing total disruption to existing services but to both the committee saw the following 'overriding' objections.

> First, it would inevitably split responsibility for the social care of individuals and families between the departments, interrupt the continuity of care, and perpetuate a symptom-centred approach. Second, and as a corollary, it would be difficult to treat the needs of an individual or family as a whole . . . In addition, such a reorganisation would offer little or no additional attraction to recruits to the services from any of the professions and no advantage over the existing situation

in attracting additional resources. There would be no major simplification of the present structure in terms of departmental organisation [1].

It pointed out that in areas where there are already combined health and welfare departments there would be the additional complication of another department.

Three further alternatives were eventually discarded—a social casework department acting on an agency basis for other departments; the personal social services absorbed into an enlarged health department or into the health and education departments; or taking the personal social services away from local government. The first was rejected on the grounds that the relationship between the public and social services agencies would still be confusing. Moreover, the problem of divided responsibility would not be overcome since this 'solution' would split the residential services from other social work services.

The second suggestion—the amalgamation of local authority social services, either into an enlarged health department or into expanded health and education departments—was opposed by the committee on the grounds that both versions failed to tackle the 'lack of resources' problem [2]. The social care services had traditionally been neglected in comparison with the health and education services. The former sector required concentrated attention which was not distracted by the demands of other kinds of service. Furthermore, a perpetuation of 'divided responsibility' [3] would result from an assimilation of social workers into the health and education departments. The last solution —removing the personal social services from local government altogether—was not considered very seriously by the committee because it was seen as outside its terms of reference.

The decision to argue for a unified department was taken only months after the committee began sitting. Draft chapter headings, which bore a remarkable similarity to those of the final report, had been circulated by September 1966. An outline draft of Chapter Five indicated clearly the committee's preference for reorganization rather than co-ordination as a solution. This chapter was to include an analysis of the problems, discussions of the case for change and a conclusion that co-ordination had 'serious drawbacks' [4].

Exact Boundaries

Having decided upon the broad organizational structure it would recommend, the committee faced two major problems. The first was the precise boundaries to be drawn around the departments and the second concerned the relationship between these new agencies and central government. If the criterion for reorganization was to be the unification of services for all those requiring social work help, which services should be included? The most important questions to be answered concerned the demarcation lines between the new department and five existing groups of services—those which were the responsibility of the local authority health, education and housing departments, the National Health Service, the Supplementary Benefits Commission and the probation service.[1] This section highlights a few of the more interesting and contentious ones.

Division of functions between the health and social services departments

The boundary between the health and social services departments was, most members argued, the hardest to define. Should the non-medical treatment of the mentally disordered be regarded as part of the National Health Service or the new departments? To which agency should mental welfare officers, psychiatric social workers, health visitors and home helps be attached? The mentally disordered so clearly required a collaborative effort between those with medical and social skills that the weakness of an attempt to divorce the two services was highlighted in this area of need. The committee decided after much heart-searching and some dissension that the mental health social services[2] should be included in the new department. Its rationale was that the social care and support of the mentally disordered should be integrated with the social services for the family.

The decision was not an easy one to reach. The medical lobby argued strongly that social work services for the mentally disordered should continue to be under the overall control of a doctor. It was pointed out that the community medical teams being formed by some local health authorities would be severely affected if their mental health services were removed. These services were the jewel in the crown of many health departments. Whilst the committee acknowledged the 'outstanding achievements' [5] of some departments, it maintained that this was no reason for preserving the status quo. Adding support to the view that the social services departments should be responsible

---

[1] The National Health Service, the Supplementary Benefits Commission and the probation service were technically outside the committee's terms of reference.

[2] With the exception of the junior training centres, the future of which was being considered at the time. These were made an education department function in 1970.

for these services was the evidence from the Association of Psychiatric Social Workers and the Institute of Medical Social Workers which argued against the health department being in charge.

Some of the enquiry's members saw the mental health issue as one which might deeply divide the committee since it involved a clash of interests between the local authority medical teams and social workers. The loyalties of the group were split on this question but the key to its resolution lay in decisions on the future of the health departments. The removal of social work services for the mentally disordered from the health authorities left a rump department which, it could be argued, was not viable as a local government agency and should be combined with the hospital and general practitioner services. Professor Morris, the only member with close medical connections, was eventually persuaded that both medical and social skills were required to meet the needs of the mentally disordered. He recognized that social work skills were vital in this area of need and was therefore prepared to see the social services departments assume responsibility for some parts of the mental health services. He was not unduly worried by the weakening of the health departments since he saw their future lying in a unified medical service.

The issue of whether a unified health service might be formed inside or outside local government was not discussed. The local government members of the committee were only willing to consider the transfer of mental health services from health departments if these departments remained workable local government units. They feared that after creating comprehensive social work departments the remaining health functions would not be considered viable and might be removed from local government altogether. If this happened the gulf between the medical and social services would be widened, thus weakening the delivery of services to those with a mixture of social and medical needs, such as the mentally disordered. The committee's report recognized the problem but disclaimed responsibility for precipitating a crisis within local health services. 'Our proposals affecting local authority health departments have done no more, we believe, than bring into the open weaknesses that have been present in them since 1948.'[1]

Less contentious than the future of the mental health social services

[1] Seebohm Report, op. cit., p. 121. The realization that proposals in the forthcoming Seebohm Report would have serious implications for the local health departments added weight to the wide pressure for a reappraisal of the N.H.S. structure. In November 1967 the Minister of Health announced that the department was to conduct an enquiry into the organization of the health

were decisions on the location of the home help and health visitor services. Concerning the former, the committee had received evidence from the home help organizers that they would prefer to operate from the health department, but the members found their views unacceptable, arguing that in the past contact between home helps and doctors had been infrequent. Located within the new department home helps would develop their full potential as a preventive service and provide 'a remedy for difficult social as well as medical situations'[6]. On this issue the committee's conclusions ran counter to the evidence from medical groups such as the British Medical Association and the Society of Medical Officers of Health as well as from the para-professional groups involved.

The members had little difficulty in making recommendations on the placing of the health visitor service. The roles of social workers and health visitors had often been confused in the past but the report argued that the distinctions should be reinforced, the latter remaining with the health departments. The decision was influenced by the fact that many health visitors combined their role with that of district nurse or midwife. The practical problems of separating these functions would have been considerable.

The social services department and the education services

In defining the boundary between the education service and the new department, the committee considered the social work services relating to children under five and those provided for children of school age. Discussion on the relationship between the proposed new departments and the education authorities took place within the general context of the Plowden Council's Report on primary schools [7]. The council stressed the importance of social work in schools and tentatively concluded that, whilst social workers in such a setting should always be immediately responsible to the head teacher for their work on behalf of the school, their administrative responsibilities should normally be to a team leader located in a service having broader social work functions. Thus social work services for children of school age presented comparatively few problems. The Seebohm Committee could, with a clear conscience, recommend that social work in schools should be encouraged and should be administered by the social services departments. Responsi-

services. The culmination of this enquiry was the publication of a green paper in July 1968. The interrelationship of planning within the health and social services fields is discussed in the next chapter.

bility for the under fives on the other hand proved a much more difficult issue to resolve.

Plowden's recommendations for the under fives were that education authorities should be responsible for providing nursery schools and nursery classes for all children between the ages of three and five whose parents wished them to attend. The Seebohm Committee accepted this proposal but argued that there would be inadequate resources to meet the demand for many years and that in any case, nursery schools only occupied a small part of the child's day and were closed for part of the year. It maintained, therefore, that the social services departments should carry responsibility for providing community care facilities during those periods when three- to five-year olds were not attending nursery schools.

The committee were so divided over the issue of pre-school provision that their report openly acknowledges the conflict [8]. The majority thought that the new department should be given responsibility for providing pre-school play-groups, whilst two members were adamant that the education department should retain this service. When drafting this part of the report, the careful representation of the divisions in opinion was important as at least one of the members would have been prepared to sign a note of dissent if an acceptable form of words had not been found. It seems a curious issue to excite such deep feelings; the committee considered so many issues which seemed to the outsider to be of similar or greater weight,[1] and yet reached a sufficient measure of agreement to present a united front in the final report. Moreover, the play-group question did not involve the committee in arbitration between sizeable professional groups as did the issue of health and social service department boundaries. It appears from discussions with the members that a disproportionate amount of the committee's time was devoted to this issue because two of the committee could not be persuaded to change their minds whilst the chairman was extremely reluctant to allow a note of dissent. The treatment of the play-group question by the committee suggests that apparently minor issues may assume greater importance and receive more attention than issues of similar weight if they threaten the cohesion of the enquiry.

Boundaries between the social services department and other services

Decisions on the demarcation lines between housing authorities and

[1] For a discussion of the weighing of issues see pp. 79–80.

the 'Seebohm departments' provided few real difficulties for the committee. The full range of housing responsibilities was to remain with the former but the provision of recuperative units and social work services for homeless families should be provided by the latter [9]. Persuaded by the logic that general responsibility for the homeless was indisputably a housing matter, the committee recommended that it should reside with the housing department. They, it was argued, were the bodies with houses to allocate.

Thornier questions were involved when debating the divisions of functions between the social services department and the Supplementary Benefits Commission (S.B.C.) and the probation service. Since consideration of both services was outside its terms of reference, the committee argued that it would discuss only the *implications* of its proposals for these services. However, its remarks concerning the S.B.C., though carefully phrased, go beyond the implications of its proposals for the work of the Commission. The major problem—a perennial one—was the desirability of attempting to retain the distinction between the provision of cash benefits and welfare services. When the S.B.C. was formed in 1966, the introduction of a 'visiting service', which would represent a considerable extension of the rudimentary welfare functions of the old N.A.B., was seriously considered. The committee looked with disfavour on this proposal, arguing that it cut across its attempts to unify social work and avoid divisions of responsibility. Indeed its report states the members' preference for a clear separation of functions in no uncertain terms.

> It seems to us [it argued] that a natural and helpful division of responsibility emerges between the Commission and the new social service department. The Commission's functions in ascertaining need and referring clients to the social service department should be helpful to both organisations and should, we believe, ensure the most effective help for the clients. We consider that the Commission's officers should refer cases to that department and should not attempt to undertake social work themselves . . . there are real dangers in providing a service of this kind through a variety of statutory sources [10].

Partly as a result of this opposition, the suggestion for a visiting service was dropped but debates about the boundary between the S.B.C. and the social services departments continue [11].

Whilst the members were united in their views on the idea of a visiting service, they found it difficult to agree on their position *vis-à-vis* the probation service. The separation of the planning process for probation from that for other social work services was discussed earlier.[1] The Home Office had ensured that the committee's terms of reference did not cover probation, yet all members agreed that some comment on the desirability of maintaining a close relationship between this service and those concerned with family welfare was necessary. However, the majority wished to discuss the relationship between the two services in more detail, an exercise which was hotly disputed by a small minority who felt that the terms of reference should be strictly interpreted.

The future provision for young offenders raised a sensitive boundary issue, to which the report alluded obliquely. 'Recent developments in aftercare and parole bring the probation and aftercare service increasingly into work in the community and thus raise the danger of unplanned overlapping' [12]. Since 1966, Home Office officials had been developing their second white paper relating to young offenders, a process which involved consideration of the social and educational aspects as well as of the purely legal ones. Clearly there could be an overlap here between the Seebohm Committee's deliberations and the planning within the Home Office. Both groups were aware of this possibility and hence the committee met Mr Derek Morell, the responsible assistant secretary at the Home Office, several times to discuss the questions involved. It was obvious that there were areas of conflict.

In 1966 the Plowden Council [13] had suggested the creation of educational priority areas (E.P.A.s) as a device for channelling extra resources to the disadvantaged child. The policy was adopted and subsequently certain civil servants within the Home Office had begun to consider the possibility of extending the principle of positive discrimination to deprived communities. Some members of the committee saw this development as an encroachment upon their terms of reference and requested that the planning of this part of the white paper be postponed until they had reported. Reluctantly it was agreed that the white paper would be published without discussion of the community development projects (C.D.P.s) then under consideration.

In its report the Seebohm Committee requested that the government should institute a review of the implications of its recommendations for probation and aftercare. Furthermore, it devoted a whole chapter to 'the community'. Here it was argued that the social services departments should play a crucial part in the development of community identity, in mobilizing local resources, in organizing voluntary effort and ensuring genuine consumer participation. The committee maintained, however,

[1] See pp. 28–9.

that for some areas of special need this effort should be supplemented and, hence, that priority areas should be singled out for the allocation of additional resources.

Very different versions of the early planning of community development ideas have emerged. Some have argued that the impetus for an extension of the Plowden policy came from the Home Office and that the Seebohm Committee's efforts in this direction delayed the establishment of the community development projects. Others interpreted Home Office interest in this field as a further attempt to limit the purview of a committee of whose existence they disapproved. Moreover, by laying claim to policies directed at the community the department was strengthening its case to take responsibility for the reorganized services suggested by the Seebohm Committee.

Central-Local Government Relationships

The precise relationship between the central authority (or authorities) and the new departments was an issue the committee found extremely difficult to resolve. There were deep divisions of opinion amongst the members as to the desirability of making recommendations which increased central control over local government. Those primarily interested in the delivery of the services under consideration stressed the need for considerable central control in order to ensure that no authorities fell below a reasonable minimum standard. On the other hand, the members with local authority interests argued that this would inhibit experimentation at a local level and, more importantly, that the limitation of local autonomy would conflict with current views on the balance of power between central and local government. They pointed to the recommendations of the Committee on the Management of Local Government (the Maud Committee) [14], where general decentralization of power was advocated.

For the Seebohm Committee, the issue had two main facets. Should its recommendations for a social services committee and for a principal officer, comparable with the chief education officer or medical officer of health, be made mandatory? Secondly should the appointment of these new chief officers be subject to ministerial approval? Before considering the details, the committee reached a collective decision that it should concentrate on the best structure for a social services department even though this might, in parts, conflict with the Maud Committee's recommendations.

It concluded that a statutory duty should be placed upon local

authorities to create a separate social services committee and a principal
officer with adequate supporting staff. The report acknowledged that
this recommendation curtailed the freedom of the individual authority
to decide upon its internal structure and conflicted with the Maud
Committee's proposals for a repeal of the legal provisions which
required authorities to establish certain committees. It was maintained
that 'the scale of current needs in the field of the personal social services
and the concentration of effort which will be needed to make good the
present deficiencies amply justify our proposal . . .' [15].

The second important aspect of this issue was the ministerial right of
veto over the appointment of individuals to chief officer posts. This
split the committee into several camps. The phrasing of the final
recommendation indicates that it was impossible to reach unanimity on
this point.

> We are all agreed [the report stated] . . . that [local authorities] should
> be required to consult the responsible minister about the composition
> of the short list and to take account of any observations he may make
> before making the appointment. The majority of us do however go
> further and recommend that a minimum requirement should be for
> ministerial approval for the first appointment and for any further
> appointment during the first twelve months; some members of the
> majority wish to see this principle extended indefinitely or until the
> new organisation is firmly established . . . [16]

Again, the committee's conclusions cut across those of the Maud
enquiry, since the latter were emphatic that all appointments to chief
officer posts should be left to the discretion of the local authority.

It is perhaps not surprising, given the committee's task to find the
machinery necessary for the delivery of an effective family service, that
on balance the members considered the status of the locally administered personal social services more important than the autonomy of
local government in general. More specifically, the rationale for a
statutory committee depended upon interpretation of the quality of the
children's and welfare services. It had been mandatory since 1948 for
local authorities to establish departments in the case of the former but
not the latter. Forty-six authorities had no separate welfare committees.
Several of the members argued that the children's services were of a
higher standard than the welfare services and that this could be
attributed to their statutory status. In fact there is very little hard
evidence to support or disprove this argument apart from the greater
proportion of trained personnel in the children's departments. In 1967
fewer than 20% of social workers within welfare departments (excluding

staff in residential institutions) had any professional qualifications for their work [17]. In contrast, about 32% of the staff working in children's departments were professionally qualified in one branch of social work and a further 21% had a university degree, diploma or certificate [18].

Specialization and Training

Alongside the major issues considered by the committee there were other questions of importance. Two such issues were crucial for the future of the social work profession. First, should the social worker specialize and, if so, along what lines and at what level; second, how should social work training be organized and financed? The difficulty facing the committee was that the answers to these questions differed according to the branch of social work with which the person or group giving evidence identified.

The evidence presented to the committee on specialization was scanty and social worker groups put forward a variety of views on whether it should be encouraged and if so, in what form.[1] The issue is interesting because, whilst the balance of evidence was in favour of continued specialization along existing or new lines, the committee concluded that 'as a general rule and as far as possible, a family or individual in need of social care should be served by a single social worker' [19]. It was recognized, however, that some elements of specialization would be necessary but the committee were unspecific about the forms this would take.

> We expect [it argued] that as the service develops specialisations will cluster differently and new types of specialisation emerge to meet new problems and needs and fresh conceptions of how they might be tackled. It would be unwise to attempt to define these now but we are clear that there ought to be someone . . . with a particular responsibility for helping with the problems of residential institutions and with social work with communities.

The decision to recommend the reduction in specialization, against the weight of the views presented, was particularly contentious. Perhaps more than any other recommendation it armed critics with 'evidence' that the primary aim of the enquiry was to develop a united social work profession.

Although there were some differences of opinion on the degree to

[1] See p. 51.

which differentiation between social workers should be reduced, on the issue of specialization the committee was fairly united. The conflicts, where they existed, were between the committee and those presenting evidence. In contrast, the organization and finance of social work training produced differences *within* the committee which mirrored those taking place between social work groups. The difficulties stemmed from the fact that the Central Training Council in Child Care (C.T.C.C.) and the Council for Training in Social Work (C.T.S.W.) had in the past operated rather differently. The former was established under the Children Act, 1948, when the Home Office was given responsibility for services to children in need. It was an integral part of the Home Office, its staff being civil servants and its policy to arrange for colleges to provide courses financed by the department. The Council for Training in Social Work was established by a special statute—the Health Visiting and Social Work (Training Act, 1962. Although its budget was allotted by the Ministry of Health, it had greater independence than the Central Training Council in Child Care. Its members were not civil servants and its chairman could refer issues to the Privy Council if agreement between the minister and the training council could not be reached. The policy of the council was to encourage polytechnics and other colleges of further education to run courses but unlike the C.T.C.C. these courses had to be financed by the educational body concerned. The experience of these two bodies suggested that the price paid for independence was greater difficulty in obtaining adequate funds. Yet, for some members of the committee and pressure groups,[1] independence with regard to decisions on training was seen as crucial. In the long term they believed it to be safer to institute courses using the normal educational programmes rather than the earmarked funds from a central department since the latter could be subject to more serious fluctuations during political crises. Moreover, at this stage in the professional development of social work it was desirable to minimize the departmental influence over the number and content of courses.

Differences between committee members tended to break along the following lines. Those familiar with the probation and child care services favoured a Training Council financed by, and working closely with, the responsible central department whilst those accustomed to the C.T.S.W. model argued for a council with greater independence. The final report, however, reflects little of this debate. Unlike the issues of pre-school provision and the relationship between central and local

[1] See p. 50.

government, where a carefully phrased difference of opinion was reflected, contentious aspects of social work training were not discussed. The report recommended that there should be one central body responsible for promoting the training of staff of the personal social services, but did not discuss questions of finance or the relationship of the new advisory council to the central department. Instead it maintained that 'the precise functions and responsibilities of the council acting through its standing committee will have to be worked out with the various bodies involved' [20].

Implementation of Reform

The committee had some difficulty in coming to conclusions on when its recommendations should be introduced. Should its report suggest awaiting local government reorganization or argue that its proposals be implemented as soon as possible? Evidence from the Association of Municipal Corporations and several other bodies had maintained that any reorganization of the personal social services should await local government reform on the grounds that 'two consecutive changes involving staff upheavals could well produce such a heavy strain on staff that the efficiency of the services might well be prejudiced' [21].

Within the committee there were differences of view on the issue. The local government members were, somewhat predictably, in favour of awaiting local government reform. Another member took a similar line, arguing for a period of experimentation before choosing a particular model. This would provide additional time to replan the health services and reduce the opposition of the medical officers of health. The remainder of the committee, however, were in favour of recommending that reform should take place as soon as was feasible since they believed that local government reorganization could take several years to effect and that a delay would reduce the likelihood of the new department ever being introduced. The latter view prevailed and the eventual form of words was unequivocal. 'Our proposals,' the report maintains, 'should be implemented as quickly as possible and without waiting for general reorganization following the recommendations of the Royal Commission on Local Government in England' [22].

London

The question of whether Greater London, which had recently undergone major local government reorganization, should be included in the committee's recommendations was discussed in the light of some evidence arguing for the exclusion of the metropolitan area. In particular, the London Boroughs Association (L.B.A.) had stressed the problems for London of a further upheaval following the reorganization which came into effect in 1965. It had commissioned a report from the London Boroughs' Management Service Unit (L.B.M.S.U.) on reorganization within London, the results of which were ready for publication by March 1968. The unit's recommendations caused a stir within the committee since they were contrary to those being finalized by the enquiry. The former proposed grouping together the local health services, the children's services and the welfare services in order to reduce the number of principal officers in the boroughs. These proposals were themselves somewhat disturbing to the committee. More important, however, was the encouragement they might give to London boroughs to reorganize *in advance* of the Seebohm recommendations. The boroughs of Greenwich and Sutton were already attempting to do so by amalgamating the children's, health and welfare services under the control of the medical officer of health.

The committee was extremely anxious to prevent such pre-empting of its recommendations. Frederic Seebohm contacted Michael Stewart, the co-ordinator of the social services,[1] and requested that a public statement condemning pre-empting should be made. On 28 March, in response to a parliamentary question from Eric Moonman, the Home Secretary expressed his disapproval of premature reorganization [23]. In addition, Seebohm wrote to the chairman of the L.B.A. and the L.B.M.S.U. asking that the report be withheld until the enquiry's proposals were published. The chairman of the latter argued that he could not delay the report since the London Boroughs Association had commissioned it and Seebohm decided not to push the matter further since the results of the report seemed generally known.

The Seebohm Report mentions the L.B.M.S.U. study only in passing. The committee was united in its view that there would be 'major disadvantages' in omitting Greater London and although it discussed the issue in committee, this was left out of the report. It did, however, acknowledge the need to make special arrangements for Inner London, where the administrative problems were unique. Here, the school enquiry and school welfare services were the responsibility of the Inner London Education Authority (I.L.E.A.), the school health

[1] Douglas Houghton was succeeded in this post by Patrick Gordon-Walker, who was followed by Michael Stewart in August 1966.

service was provided jointly by the boroughs and the I.L.E.A., and the children's, health, welfare and part of the housing service were in the hands of the boroughs. The report recommended a compromise scheme—social services departments at borough level should be responsible for social care in the community and therefore for seconding social workers to schools, but the school psychological service should remain in the hands of the I.L.E.A.

Scotland

The developments within Scotland merit detailed study in their own right but only those aspects which had implications for the Seebohm Committee are discussed here. We noted earlier[1] that in July 1965 the Scottish Office appointed a small advisory group to work with civil servants on the reappraisal of their local authority social services including the probation service. This planning process produced a white paper by 1966 [24] and the Act based upon it by July 1968 (the same month as the Seebohm Report was published) [25]. In Scotland there was only one central department—the Scottish Office—involved. More than any other single factor this explains the speed with which change was achieved. It meant that there were no major interdepartmental struggles to contend with, and although the sevices had developed nuclei of prefossional vested interests around them, these were weaker than those in England. The civil servants of the Scottish Home and Health Department worked closely with the advisory group. Moreover, they had the enthusiastic support of the Under Secretary, Judith Hart.

The Social Work (Scotland) Act created local authority social work departments similar in many respects to those proposed by the Seebohm Committee. One might have expected that many of the issues faced in Scotland would have been of interest to the committee since similar questions were likely to arise for them. The delineation of the boundaries, the relationship between central and local government, the heads of the new departments, the future of the medical officer of health—these were all issues faced in Scotland and subsequently ones to be considered by the Seebohm Committee. Events in Scotland were discussed by the group and they had a brief meeting with representatives of the Scottish Home and Health Department after considering a draft of their white paper. There is only passing reference to Scotland in the report, however [26], and some of those involved in the Scottish

[1] See pp. 25–6.

decision-making process maintained that, at the time, they were disappointed at the lack of interest shown by the committee and the social services ministries at Whitehall.[1]

Packaging the Report

Any enquiry must make decisions, explicit or otherwise, on the best way to present and 'sell' its product. Frederic Seebohm was well aware of the importance of careful presentation and took certain tactical decisions as a result. He made it quite clear to the committee that he would be most reluctant to accept a minority report or notes of dissent. The alternatives are to omit contentious issues from the final report, to find a suitably bland form of words or to set out the division of opinion between the members in the main report. Seebohm chose to use all of these alternatives: the future of the child guidance service was not discussed in much detail because it was a contentious but fairly minor issue for the committee; the passage relating to the probation services required careful phraseology; and the pre-school play-group issue plus that of central-local relationships necessitated making explicit the divisions of opinion between the members.

Seebohm wished to present a report which would be both eminently practical for policy-makers and comprehensible to the layman. It was decided, therefore, to omit some of the philosophical discussion which took place within the committee. As we have seen, several papers were produced on such topics as the concept of a family service [27] and the function of social work [28]. They formed an important part of the committee's deliberations and some members felt that they should have been included. Certainly much of the subsequent criticism of the report centred around the lack of discussion of basic issues such as the concepts of 'need' and 'effectiveness' and the function of social work within a societal context.

A further decision taken by the members was about the extent to which they should attempt to estimate the resource implications of their proposals. The Plowden Council had provided fairly detailed estimates of the costs of their proposals regarding nursery and primary education. They predicted that the implementation of their recommendations would result in an increase in the total current costs of these sectors of 8% by 1972/3 and 14% by 1978/9 [29]. It was argued, however, that most of the additional resources could be found by the diversion

[1] Several added that this was unexceptional in that events in Scotland rarely attract interest South of the border!

of expenditure from other areas of education. Thus, the council came down in favour of attempting to cost their recommendations but keeping the bill as low as possible. Maurice Kogan, who was the secretary for the committee argues that there was 'no coherent pattern of action on or reaction to its conclusions' [30]. Exactly how the specification or otherwise of resource implications will affect the reception of a report is impossible to determine. It must remain largely a matter of political guesswork.

Frederic Seebohm decided that the best strategy for his committee to adopt was to keep the financial and manpower implications of its proposals vague. This resulted in the adoption of a somewhat contradictory stance. It was argued that an effective family service could not be provided without an increase in resources [31]; indeed, one of the main reasons for proposing a unified department was to attract additional resources for the personal social services. Yet, despite this explicit objective, the financial implications of such a policy were not fully developed. The only estimates of social service department expenditure were based upon the simple aggregation of the existing costs of the individual services to be included in the new department.

The committee maintained that the departments' budgets would be about 46% higher than the combined expenditure of children's and welfare services, the additional outlay being accounted for by expensive services not previously provided by either of these departments, for example, home helps and parts of the mental health services. Regarding manpower, the report argued that a 'modest increase' in social workers could 'affect significantly the effectiveness of a family service' [32]. Moreover, it maintained that a reduction in the numbers of children and old people taken into residential care could result in some financial economies. The intention of the committee was, above all, to ensure that reorganization took place even if, initially, it was achieved without attracting additional resources from central government. The second battle could be joined once reorganization was effected. In retrospect it seems probable that their judgement on the resources question was politically sound. The reorganization of the personal social services was introduced with no additional expenditure allowed for in the Act. It is unlikely that these changes would have taken place at all had debate focused upon the expansion of resources in addition to administrative reform.[1]

---

[1] This argument is developed on p. 103.

Selling the Report

Some enquiries take deliberate steps to ensure that their proposals are previewed by feeding material to the press in advance of publication, but the Seebohm Committee as a whole decided against such a tactic. Although they decided collectively to keep silence until the report itself was ready, however, *The Guardian* of 4 May 1968 carried an article 'predicting' with great accuracy the enquiry's recommendations. Since it seemed likely that the reporter had gained access to the committee's minutes, this particular leak, far from letting the members in gently to public reaction, created additional tensions during the difficult final drafting period.

Once a committee's report is complete most members of enquiries are content to consider their part in the policy-making process at an end but not so in the case of the Seebohm Committee. The members were so committed to the conclusions of their report that most of them felt it was necessary to publicize their proposals by 'stomping' the country. They met many groups, some of them initially very hostile, to discuss the ideas contained in the report. It was clear that a number of social workers still needed convincing on the broad conclusions of the report and certainly required clarification on some of the more complex areas such as the meaning of a reduction in specialization. Some of the meetings were uncomfortably lively for the members as many medical officers of health took the opportunity to criticize them in person for their biased opinions and lack of foresight. As far as one can tell this extension of a committee's role is unique in the history of enquiries.

Discussion

The way in which the Seebohm Committee defined the basic problems of the personal social services—the lack of resources, inadequate knowledge and divided responsibility—placed important constraints upon the conclusions reached. A large department was, in their view, necessary to attract resources and develop the planning capability to assess needs. Moreover, if divided responsibility was a major weakness, then solutions which involved the co-ordination of more than one department employing social workers were unlikely to be chosen.

The decision to recommend a unified department was reached fairly early on. It had to be taken before decisions on boundaries and the relationship between central and local government departments could be made. Yet draft headings for the whole report had been circulated by September 1966. The dates on which evidence was presented indicate that some groups were clearly too late to influence the committee on whether or not to form a unified department. A second reason given as to why the evidence was not very helpful when deciding this issue was that the better evidence in terms of argument and presentation confirmed the enquiry's early views. This argument is, of course, dangerously circular; the 'better' evidence may have appeared to be superior because it confirmed the members' own opinions.

Whilst the evidence contributed little to the taking of the main decisions, it was more important when the committee considered other issues, notably the boundaries question and the relationship between central and local government, but also specialization, training and the introduction of reforms.

Summarizing the contribution from the major groups involved, it can be said that the ministries' evidence added little to the committee's understanding of the problems involved and possible solutions to them. Their contribution suffered from the need to restrict their suggestions to those services for which they had responsibility at the time. It is interesting in retrospect, however, because it underlines the point that departments are not composed of homogeneous groups of civil servants. The issues discussed by the Seebohm Committee presented conflicts not only *between* ministries but *within* them, especially in the case of the Ministry of Health where health and welfare interests clashed.

Evidence from the social work organizations appears to have been of use to the committee not because it convinced them that a unified department was necessary but because it confirmed the enquiry's early views. It also provided important information on the opinions of some practitioners and especially on the differences between and within branches of social work over certain issues such as specialization and training. The evidence from medical groups was, on the whole, unhelpful, in part because it was poorly argued but, more particularly, because some organizations argued against change whilst others proposed radical reorganization. It was, therefore, impossible to respond favourably to them all. The local government evidence was, like that from the medical groups, difficult to process and it omitted any discussion of a key issue for the committee—that of central-local relationships. Nevertheless, it underlined the need to consider possible changes in local government structures and the fact that reorganization of the personal social services presented conflicts not only between central departments but, at local authority level, between chief officers.

So far no account has been taken of *oral evidence*. This omission is due to the fact that for the researcher this part of the process is extremely difficult to cover unless it is possible to draw freely upon the minutes of the committee in question. Even then these often provide only brief, bland comments about the proceedings. A couple of points concerning the oral evidence to Seebohm are, however, worth noting. In its educational role the committee felt that it was important to establish its credibility with interest groups where possible. It deliberately conducted the receipt of oral evidence, therefore, on neutral ground in accommodation provided by the Ministry of Housing and Local Government despite the fact that the rooms were rather unwelcoming. Once these sessions were finished, most of the meetings were held at the National Institute for Social Work Training. The presentation of oral evidence served to modify, clarify and to expand the written documents submitted. A particularly clear example of modification can be seen in the evidence presented by the Association of Children's Officers and Association of Child Care Officers. Both groups suggested in their written evidence that reform should be implemented in phases[1] but by the time their representatives met the committee they had decided to abandon that proposal.

Unsurprisingly, the views of the members themselves were probably the most important single factor influencing the committee's conclusion. Although the membership was recruited from a limited 'universe', the individuals selected brought to the committee very varied opinions on a number of issues.[2] Determining the relative importance of issues is extremely difficult. There was considerable agreement amongst the members as to which were the major issues; the boundaries question as a whole and, in particular, the demarcation line between the health and personal social services, were usually mentioned first, followed by the extent of ministerial control over local government. As one would expect, however, since the members were chosen in part for their special interests, most of them cherished one or more issues which did not excite great interest amongst the rest. Sometimes the members could agree amongst themselves but did not accept the majority view presented in evidence. Two examples of this were the questions of whether London should be included in the proposals[3] and whether the home help service should be located in the new department.[4]

Certain debates generated particularly strong feelings, amongst them the location of the mental health and pre-school services, ministerial

[1] See pp. 49–50.
[2] See Appendix Three.
[3] See pp. 72–4.
[4] See pp. 63–4.

control and the timing of reforms. Some of these were considered important by all the members; some like the pre-school issue were not. Evidence from the Seebohm Committee suggests that where one or two members are prepared to reject the majority view, even a minor question may consume a disproportionate amount of time. Given these differences of opinion it is perhaps surprising that the report exhibits a fairly high degree of consensus. How was this achieved? The effect of group pressures was one factor; there were only ten members. This meant that time could be spent in full committee persuading recalcitrant members to adopt the majority viewpoint. In the case of allocating responsibility for the services for the mentally disordered, careful persuasion was successful. In that of the location of pre-school play-groups, it failed.

5 The Political Arena

The period from July 1968 to August 1969 was one of great activity for politicians, civil servants and pressure groups concerned with all aspects of the social services. The planning processes set in motion by the Labour government in its early years of office were beginning to show results. In April 1968 the white paper outlining the government's proposals for the treatment of young offenders and the Report of the Royal Commission on Medical Education [1] were produced. Later, in July, the Social Work (Scotland) Act was passed and the same month the Seebohm Report and a green paper suggesting a possible framework for the reorganization of the National Health Service [2] were published. Meanwhile, the Royal Commission on the reform of local government was considering changes which would profoundly affect the delivery of many social services.

In the autumn of 1964, Harold Wilson had recognized the need for close working relationships between central departments in planning for housing, education, health, social security and the personal social services by introducing a co-ordinator of social services. Several senior ministers subsequently held the office—Douglas Houghton, Patrick Gordon-Walker, Michael Stewart and, lastly, Richard Crossman. It became clear fairly quickly, however, that this machinery was inadequate, lacking as it did financial and executive powers. In April 1968 another attempt to facilitate coherent planning was announced. The Ministry of Social Security and the Ministry of Health were to be combined in the following November under the overlordship of Richard Crossman whose formal title was to be not Secretary of State for Health and Social Security but Secretary of State for Social Services.

The timing and eventual provisions of the Local Authority Social Services Act, 1970, can largely be explained by four factors:
   the timing and nature of planning in related fields;
   the strategies of pressure groups;
   the influence of individuals; and
   the general election of June 1970.

The complex inter-relationship of the planning processes, and especially that between the health service and personal social services, is best conveyed by examining the most important developments chronologically. The Seebohm Report and the government's first green paper on the reorganization of the National Health Service came out on the same day, to facilitate simultaneous consideration of changes spanning both the health and personal social services. Clearly issues such as the boundaries between social work and medicine, the future of the medical officer of health, and the timing of reforms were ones which required co-ordinated planning and thus the future of the Seebohm Committee's proposals was dependent, in part, upon the fortunes of health service planning.

Reactions to 'Seebohm' and the Green Paper (July – December 1968)

The political response to Seebohm

In the past it has been fairly widely supposed that the social services generally, but particularly the welfare services, are a backwater of political life, exciting little interest amongst senior politicians and not one of the steps on the ladder to the highest posts. It is perhaps surprising, therefore, that the Seebohm proposals were given very serious consideration by the full Cabinet and generated extremely strong, if adverse, reactions. The Prime Minister gave the report the usual ritual welcome in the Commons on its publication day, but announced that no decisions would be made until consultations had been undertaken [3].

A few days later the Cabinet discussed the proposals and Richard Crossman's diaries record that the report's reception was very unfavourable. 'Everybody said it was a contemptible report,' he wrote but sadly he does not give any reasons for such a response. According to Crossman's account they discussed whether to reject the proposals immediately but decided instead to refer them to the Cabinet's Social Services Sub-committee. Crossman suggests that the feeling of the meeting was that the reorganization of the personal social services might well be appropriate but that the committee had not put forward a watertight case for such a development.

One of the Seebohm Report's suggestions—that a single central department should be given responsibility for the personal social services—was dismissed fairly quickly. The two obvious departments to which primary responsibility for these services could be given were the

Home Office and the Ministry of Health (soon to become the Department of Health and Social Security). However, neither James Callaghan, Secretary of State for the Home Office, nor Richard Crossman, who was then Secretary of State designate for the Social Services, was prepared to give up any of the services for which they were responsible. Crossman saw the new enlarged D.H.S.S. as the obvious location for the personal social services. Callaghan, on the other hand, was anxious to protect the children's services since the Home Office had a good reputation for administration in this field and without these services the department was reduced in size and restricted in scope to functions of a primarily social control nature. Moreover, his department had recently received a fillip. In preference to the D.H.S.S. it had been given responsibility for co-ordinating the urban aid programme which was designed to channel additional resources to areas with particularly acute social problems.

Many of those involved, civil servants, politicians and professionals, have observed that traditional departmental conflicts were exacerbated by the long-standing political rivalry between Callaghan and Crossman. Crossman's diaries recall their antagonism in 1965 when he was Minister of Housing and Local Government and Callaghan was Chancellor of the Exchequer. 'Callaghan is curiously schizophrenic about me,' Crossman wrote, with his usual candour. 'He regards me as able and, in certain senses, someone he can talk to and understand. But he also knows that departmentally I am a fearful menace to him, and he is constantly trying to organise other members of the Cabinet against me' [4]. The only solution was a compromise; in late September 1968, Crossman enlisted Callaghan's support for replanning the personal social services on the understanding that the children's sector did not leave the Home Office until the latter's term as Home Secretary had ended. In the event, the children's services were transferred to the D.H.S.S. soon after the Conservatives were returned to power in June 1970.

The Seebohm Report was published before Crossman officially became Secretary of State for the Social Services. In his capacity as Lord President of the Council, however, he was able to use his small 'office' to work on the collation of reactions to the report. As the individual on whom the final decisions regarding the future of the health and personal social services rested, Crossman's own reactions to the Seebohm Report were important. He has said subsequently that he found the document both boring and unconvincing [5]. It is true that his many preoccupations did not include the social work services. For some years he had been involved in devising a major new pensions scheme—a project which he later formally handed over to David Ennals, Minister of State at the D.H.S.S. As Minister of Housing and Local Government for two years he had developed a keen interest in the reform of local government and in the proposals for all-purpose, unitary authorities along the lines finally suggested by the Royal Commission on Local Government. Moreover, he strongly believed that, ultimately, the future of the health service lay within local government. Crossman had to be convinced by careful argument that the personal social services constituted an activity or a set of activities which merited a local department with status comparable with that of education or housing. He felt that the Seebohm Committee failed to justify social work, accepting it instead as a self-evident good. Second, its proposals, if implemented, weakened his chances of retaining the health services within local government since it argued for the transfer of some existing health department functions to the new social services departments, thus emasculating the former. Third, he felt that the committee had been unrealistic about the cost of its proposals. His reactions are rather ironic considering the careful thought devoted by the committee to the presentation of its report and its final decision not to spend long on philosophical and definitional questions and to leave the resource implications vague.

Crossman's response to the Seebohm Committee's proposals seems all the more final given his views on the tactics of the successful minister. In a lecture given in 1970 he commented:

> Having asserted your authority, the next thing is to select a very few causes and fight for them. The greatest danger for a radical minister is to get too much going in his department. Because, you see, departments are resistant . . . There's a limit to the quantity of change they can digest. Select a few, a very few issues and on those issues be bloody and blunt because, of course, you get no change except by fighting [6].

The personal social services did not raise issues for which Crossman felt it was worth fighting.

Press reaction towards Seebohm

In general, press reaction was much warmer than that of Crossman and his colleagues. The *Economist* welcomed the committee's report but was afraid that the future of its proposals would be affected by the emphasis given to the reorganization of the National Health Service and the demands of the medical profession.

Unfortunately, it is already apparent that these on the whole eminently sensible proposals are at the mercy of the kind of professional and interdepartmental rivalries that have prevented a rational structure in the past. They must not be allowed to impede progress now. Essentially the green paper and the Seebohm Report complement each other. But the Ministry of Health rushed out its proposals to soothe the feelings of the medical officers of health whose existing functions and status would be increasingly eroded by the implementation of the Seebohm proposals. The Government ought not to succumb to pressure to put the doctors in charge of the amalgamated personal social services [7].

Surprisingly, in view of later reaction from those interested in education services, the *Times Educational Supplement* reacted favourably to the approach of the report. The leader maintained

What is needed is not an attack on the symptoms of inequality, the grammar school, the public school or Oxford but the eradication of the conditions which produce inequality early in life . . . The government should take note of the urgency of this task which the committee is at such pains to stress [8].

The Times leader welcomed both the green paper and the Seebohm Report but felt that a more logical arrangement of responsibilities, by which they meant the personal social services being placed within Mr Crossman's department, would be held up 'in the thickets of Whitehall and Westminster rivalries'.

Pressure group response to 'Seebohm'

Whilst press reaction to both Seebohm and the green paper was favourable, the response from the pressure groups involved was less so. In August 1968, a week after the publication of both documents, a press notice was issued, requesting interested bodies to make their views known to the Lord President's Office by 30 November that year. A large number of organizations—110 in all—replied. Although parts of the report were welcomed by most groups, important criticisms were levelled by doctors, the local government associations and, at this stage, even social workers.

Immediate reactions in the medical press were mixed but most expressed surprise and rejected the committee's main proposals. The *Lancet*'s comments were favouable. 'Inevitably,' it was argued, 'radical proposals disturb and threaten. But experience with the Scottish white paper suggests that balanced consideration and a readiness to rethink may be the best way for doctors to win the opportunity to make their full contribution towards an effective family service' [9]. Perhaps not surprisingly, as the trade union journal for the B.M.A., the *British Medical Journal*'s leader was much more critical. It argued that the committee showed little understanding of how the family doctor deals with social and medical problems and of his potential to lead a team dealing with personal difficulties. Regarding the leadership question, the article maintained:

> Doctors believe that this is their responsibility and ask only for the chance to have the staff to get on with the job. The public would almost certainly agree with them . . . Whatever social scientists may believe, when in trouble patients turn first to their doctor . . . [10]

Last, the article argues that the committee made light of the important issue of confidentiality. From now on one of the major arguments used against the committee's recommendations by the doctors was that confidential information given to doctors could not be divulged to social workers and therefore a medical officer would have to lead any newly formed team.

Public Health, the journal of the Society of Medical Officers of Health, analysed the power struggle behind the committee prior to the publication of the report.

> There are social workers who refuse to contemplate a situation in which they might receive instructions from a doctor and social scientists who have still too little confidence in their own science to expose it to on-the-spot criticism from colleagues in other disciplines . . . There are socialists who believe that the London School of Economics is the sacred mountain from which—and only from which—descends all wisdom. There are other socialists who see all doctors as a privileged group of the bourgeoisie trying to hold the working class to ransom . . . It would be nothing short of a tragedy if anti-doctor feeling or anti-anyone-else feeling should cause the country to be committed to an unbalanced social service policy . . . [11]

The formal evidence was more specific about the weaknesses of the report. In its submission to the Lord President's Office, the Society of Medical Officers of Health made a number of points which added up to a rejection of the committee's proposals. The Society regretted the main conclusions of the report; it urged that any decision should await the Royal Commission on Local Government and reactions to the green paper and finally it argued that implementation of the Seebohm proposals would be difficult because of the shortages of skilled social workers [12].

The Public Health Committee of B.M.A. was equally critical of the report, but spelt out its reservations more precisely. First, whilst acknowledging that it was vital to attract additional finance and staff to the health and social services, it maintained that this was not a valid reason for a social services department. Much could be achieved without organizational changes. Second, the Public Health Committee argued that, although the Seebohm Committee put great stress on co-ordination, its proposals merely created new barriers. A family approach resulted in the splitting of functional services such as those relating to mental health and thus Seebohm's solution separated health from social care. Third, the deficiencies of the health services were, it claimed, exaggerated and the preventive aspects underplayed. In particular, the committee argued that Seebohm's decisions on the location of the mental health services were arbitrary. 'What is said about the mental health service seems a clear example of the prior determination of Seebohm to justify the setting up of social service departments i.e. there is no real argument for transferring the mental health service in the community but because they want a social services department they propose to put mental health in it' [13]. Fourth, the government was strongly urged to await the Royal Commission on Local Government. Finally, the confidentiality argument was reiterated. 'The professions supplementary to medicine are known to have their own ethical codes but full co-operation will be jeopardised . . . if there is any departure from the exchange of medical information on a doctor to doctor basis.'

Reactions from the local authority associations were mixed. Both the County Councils' Association and the Association of Municipal Corporations were somewhat reluctant to react to the report before the publication of the Royal Commission on Local Government but agreed to make preliminary comments provided this did not preclude further consultation at a later stage. The C.C.A. gave a guarded welcome to the committee's proposals, agreeing with the principle of unified local authority social services but, possibly to placate the county medical officers, it made the reservation that 'the importance and scope of the local health authority services . . . have been insufficiently stressed' [14]. Perhaps surprisingly, the association felt that decisions on *some* of the main Seebohm recommendations could be put into effect before major local government reorganization.

The A.M.C., whilst agreeing with the broad philosophy of the report, had two definite objections to its proposals. The first concerned the relationship between the ministry and the new local departments. The association argued that no statutory departments or committees should be imposed on local government on the grounds that authorities should be free to experiment. Moreover, the appointment of chief officers should be a local decision with no intervention by the minister. Second, it reiterated its position that no reorganization should take place before local government reform.

The Rural District Councils' Association was the most critical of the local authority associations, viewing the committee's recommendations with 'great concern'. At that time, the association was fighting a losing battle to try to retain a district-level tier of local government responsible for at least some important services. It is not surprising, therefore, that it was alarmed by the suggestion to concentrate welfare services in a large department, thus inevitably elevating them to higher tiers of government than district authorities. The association stressed citizen participation and the importance of retaining close connections with the localities, and rejected the committee's suggestion for decentralization into area teams as 'encouraging bureaucratic developments' without 'preventing the disadvantages of remoteness' [15].

The social work press was, of course, delighted by the proposals for a unified department. In *Social Work*, David Donnison referred to the report as 'a great state paper' [16]. But having, in a sense, won their most important battle, the social workers were anxious to begin discussing the details. The Standing Conference of Organisations of Social Workers met twice to consider the report they should send to the Lord President's Office and it was decided that a general statement would be submitted. Individual groups were asked to prepare their own comments where there was disagreement. In its evidence to Crossman the conference welcomed the proposals and urged the government to introduce legislation as soon as possible. Not surprisingly, it agreed with the committee that the head of the new department should be professionally trained in social work or residential care.[1] It strongly supported the argument for ministerial control of senior appointments, but suggested that this control should be 'extended indefinitely or until the minister responsible prescribes qualifications for the post'.

These first few sentences of the statement indicate the two major preoccupations of the social work groups; if it was left to local authorities to decide, medical officers might be appointed to head these departments and, second, local government reform might delay implementation and the longer the delay, the greater the possibility of

---

[1] The committee had stressed that the new chief officers should be qualified social workers and should have received training in management and administration at appropriate points in their careers.

compromises to meet the doctors' demands or even the total rejection of
the proposals. On the question of timing the conference changed its
stance. Its evidence to the Seebohm Committee reflected the need for a
compromise position; the variations of opinion between social work
groups on important issues had resulted in a suggestion from the
conference for a period of experimentation and a phased introduction
of the new departments. Since then, however, it had become clear that
local government reform could delay the implementation of the
committee's report and that, meanwhile, pre-empting by individual
authorities, which had already begun, could take place on a massive
scale. Hence, the conference decided to abandon their proposals for
experimentation and press for a rapid and comprehensive reorganization.

The most important issue arising *between* the social work groups
concerned training arrangements. As noted earlier,[1] in the evidence to
the committee, training was a bone of contention. Subsequently,
discussion of the report itself failed to resolve the issue. Many social
workers, as embryonic professionals, saw their control of the content
and finance of training as crucial. Yet some social workers doubted
whether the profession was ready for this degree of control and,
more important, whether additional finance would be forthcoming
for an independent council. On a majority vote, the conference decided
to reject the committee's proposal for a council closely linked to a
government department. It recommended 'the establishment of an
autonomous Council for Social Work Education whose main function
would be to co-operate with other training courses and bodies in
stimulating the establishment to maintain standards necessary for
qualification from these courses'.[2] The conference stressed that
adequate grant aid should be made for this. Predictably, the Association
of Child Care Officers disassociated themselves from this suggestion,
their official policy being to implement a new council with a close
relationship to the responsible central government department, in
other words a council very similar to the existing Central Training
Council in Child Care.

Two other contentious issues between social work groups concerned
specialization and probation. The Association of Psychiatric Social
Workers was particularly critical of the committee's rather vague
comments on the degree and nature of specialization in future social

[1] See p. 50 and pp. 71–2.
[2] The model was adopted in 1971 when the Central Council for Education
and Training in Social Work was established.

work and thought that this weakness was particularly noticeable in the report's discussion of the child guidance service. The second issue centred around the official conference position regarding the location of probation officers. The National Association of Probation Officers tried to resist any reconsideration of the issue, fearing that it might lead to suggestions for including probation officers within the new departments as in Scotland. In the event the conference took no position on this and it was left to both groups to present their respective cases to the Lord President's Office. Thus the Standing Conference presented the consensus position of its member organizations, leaving the more contentious issues to become clear as individual groups made their views known.

This first round of official reactions by the major interest groups concerned presented a confused picture with no very clear allegiances emerging. There were three main dimensions to the debate—the shape of reorganization, the control of the departments and the timing of reform. On the question of the exact *form of the reorganization*, the social workers and major local authority associations—the C.C.A. and A.M.C.—were broadly in favour of the committee's proposals whereas the medical profession and the R.D.C.A. were against. Over the *control of departments* there was a different division, with the doctors and the A.M.C. opposed to strict ministerial controls, the C.C.A. undeclared and the social workers very much in favour of greater centralized direction than the committee proposed. The *timing* issue produced yet another division, with the A.M.C. and medical profession firmly against any changes in social work prior to local government reform, the C.C.A. in favour of some innovations before then and the social workers pressing for total reorganization of the personal social services before the reorganization of local government.

Reactions to the green paper on the National Health Service

Opinions on the Seebohm Report were, at this stage, rather less important than those relating to the government's green paper on the health service. The latter proposed that the tripartite structure of the N.H.S. should be replaced by an integrated administration—the basic units being 80–90 area boards—responsible for the hospital, general practitioner and existing health authority services. Whereas initial reactions to Seebohm had been mixed, those to the green paper were generally unfavourable. The B.M.A.—the single pressure group which really counted in this case—rejected the proposals outright, thus forcing a complete reappraisal of the government's plan in this field. Since the Seebohm proposals, local government reform and the future of the health service had to be developed in conjunction with each other, rejection of the green paper meant delays all round.

By the beginning of 1969 the failure of the green paper became apparent. In December 1968, the Council of the B.M.A. had drawn up a report on the reactions of the association to the government's plans, and this was agreed by a special representative meeting in January. The report concluded unequivocally that 'the main proposals enunciated in the green paper are unacceptable to the profession as a means of achieving unification of the National Health Service'. Furthermore, the report made it clear that the association would place a very high priority on new plans for community medicine and the retention of social workers as subordinates within any medical team. It stated that 'the objective of any change must be the importance of the service for the community' and that 'there must be medical supervision of all social work services with a predominantly health content and purpose . . .' [17] Commenting on the report a leader in the *British Medical Journal* maintained that 'Mr Crossman could hardly ignore the doctor's strong objections to the green paper' [18]. Less than a month later Crossman announced in a speech in Norwich that the government would be scrapping their plans and that another green paper would be produced in the autumn.

Waiting for Maud (January – July 1969)

The Seebohm lobby forms

In January 1969, the future of the Seebohm proposals looked somewhat bleak. It was clear to the social work organizations that legislation could not be passed during the current parliamentary session. The rejection of the first N.H.S. green paper meant inevitable delays and, what was worse, the B.M.A. seemed to be placing much greater emphasis on community medicine and the use of social workers in medical teams. Negotiations on a second green paper could result in a compromise much more favourable to the medical profession. The introduction of the social service departments was being further threatened by local attempts to reorganize along anti-Seebohm lines by putting the medical officer of health in charge of the social work services. The fact that no statement indicating the government's views on the subject was forthcoming reinforced social workers' fears. In January Mr Crossman replied to the questions of several M.P.s that the government were giving the comments on Seebohm 'close and careful study' [19] but he refused to be drawn further. It was at this low point that two developments of great importance for the pro-Seebohm lobby occurred.

First, Baroness Serota, who had been a member of the Seebohm Committee and who was heavily committed to the report's main conclusions, was made Minister of State (Health) in the Department of Health and Social Security.[1] Interestingly, this appointment which was so crucial for the future of the personal social services was made for reasons entirely unconnected with them. Crossman knew of Baroness Serota's work as a member of the London County Council, as chairman for many years of the L.C.C. Children's Committee and as a member of a hospital management committee. He felt she would make a good minister but later said that he had not realized until after she had been appointed that she had been a member of the Seebohm Committee [20]. From her position within the department, as the minister with responsibility for the health services, it was not easy for Baroness Serota to promote the integration of the personal social services since these were not her prime concern. Nevertheless, her influence was important because some of the decisions taken on health service reorganization inevitably affected the personal social services. Moreover, speed was essential; the enactment of the personal social services reform might well have been delayed beyond the general election if Crossman had not been persuaded by civil servants in the welfare divisions of his department and by Baroness Serota to consider the Seebohm Report's proposal fairly rapidly [21].

Second, partly because of the doctor's rejection of the green paper but more directly as a result of the threat of fairly widespread preempting, the social work groups resolved to step up their campaign. The initiative for this came from the Association of Child Care Officers, several members of which had been active in social work politics for some time. In January 1969, the A.C.C.O. called a general meeting of those bodies interested in forming a pressure group with greater scope for action and a wider membership than the Standing Conference of Organisations of Social Workers. The response was encouraging; in all, members of seventeen groups attended including representatives of the eight Standing Conference organizations, chief officer groups, voluntary and other bodies such as the Child Poverty Action Group. It was at this

[1] Baroness Serota fully supported the committee's conclusions although she did not sign the report because she left to become Baroness-in-Waiting in April 1968 before the final draft was completed.

meeting that the Seebohm Implementation Action Group (S.I.A.G.) was formed. Finance was obtained from several sources, including the Joseph Rowntree Memorial Trust.[1] The accent was on action and simplicity; the group set out to publicize their views as widely as possible through lobbying M.P.s, organizing demonstrations, issuing publicity handouts and so on.[2] Its message was unambiguous, embodying all those statements which could be made uncontroversially and categorically by all social workers. It advocated one central department (without specifying which one since there was disagreement over this), the unification of social workers into one local department and implementation of the Seebohm proposals as quickly as possible.

The formation of the S.I.A.G. was accompanied in January 1969 by other signs of impatience at the lack of government reaction to the Seebohm proposals. On the 29th the House of Lords debated the issues raised by the report, and several peers including Baroness Brooke, the Lord Bishop of Leicester, Lord James and even the Lords Platt and Amulree, eminent members of the medical profession, pressed for a government commitment. The official reply from Lord Stonham, Minister of State at the Home Office, was reserved in tone. He made it clear that, whilst the government were anxious to discourage pre-empting, they would resist pressure to react in advance of decisions in other fields. 'We do not think it right on account of these anxieties to try to take piece-meal decisions in this complex of problems without chewing and weighing up the other elements' [22]. He continued by outlining some of the difficulties to be faced: 'What about the local authorities in which health and welfare have already been merged for some time . . .? Are these links going to be broken? I think that it would be unfortunate if they were.' It was clear from his statement that no decisions had been taken and that none would be made for several months.

The opposition to Seebohm

Whilst Crossman prevaricated, the views of the anti-Seebohm lobby were being increasingly publicized. In May 1969, *Public Health*, the official Journal of the Society of Medical Officers of Health, carried an article which predicted that medical officers would lose their existing posts in the forthcoming reorganizations.

---

[1] Funds from this source were only to be spent upon the collection of information and publicity.

[2] An example of their publicity material is included as Appendix Four.

It is possible [the article argued] that the final pattern will be in some degree shaped by considerations which are mainly political . . . The doctrinaire sociologist lobby can be appeased only by the early implementation of some of the Seebohm recommendations . . . From all this it seems virtually certain that the doctors at present working for the local authorities will all or nearly all be taken into the new health service structure . . . The Medical Officer of Health will cease to exist in his present form. To soothe him it is desirable that he should have some fine-sounding title—'Community Physician' might have an imposing ring in some ears [23].

The medical officers clearly felt somewhat bitter that they had not received more support from their medical colleagues; the article continued by criticizing the Public Health Committee of the B.M.A. for their views on the future of the medical officer. It attacked the argument put by the latter that the child health and school health duties of medical officers could gradually be taken over by general practice.

In June 1969, the Society of Medical Officers of Health met Richard Crossman and Baroness Serota for what they described as 'a preliminary exchange of views'.[1] At the meeting the society's representatives made it quite clear that they were fundamentally opposed to a separation of health and personal social services but this was the last time they put this view. They realized that despite Crossman's personal predilection for the entire health service to become a local government responsibility, there were powerful arguments and powerful organizations, including other medical groups, against this view and they predicted that future plans for the health service would almost certainly involve the incorporation of existing local authority health services into a separate administrative structure. They accepted too that the proposal to establish social service departments was almost certain to be implemented. As a result, by 30 July the group had modified its tactics. A letter was circulated to its members informing them that they must be prepared for the implementation of the Seebohm Report and suggesting that, instead of outright opposition, their primary task at that point should be to make out a good case for retaining existing health authority responsibilities within the health service.

Another anti-Seebohm lobby during this period comprised those with interests in education. In January 1969 the annual report of the National Union of Teachers advisory committee for approved schools, social

[1] The files of the Society of Medical Officers of Health document this and subsequent meetings fairly fully.

welfare schools and remand homes recorded several dissenting views from both the recommendations of the government's white paper, *Children in Trouble*, and their endorsement by the Seebohm Committee [24]. The N.U.T. advisory committee disagreed with the term 'community home' for approved schools, remand homes, detention centres and special schools, since it underemphasized the educational aspect of these institutions. It was felt that the term 'social education centre' would be more appropriate. At the same time the Inner London Educational Authority was expressing strong opposition to several of the report's suggestion for integration. The Seebohm Report had proposed that social service departments at borough level should be responsible for seconding social workers to schools but the authority maintained that this would lead to duplication and muddle—the very evils the committee wished to avoid. The authority argued that many children crossed borough boundaries to go to school and could therefore be the responsibility of different social workers when at home and when at school. In support of this view it produced a plan which argued for the integration of the I.L.E.A.'s school care and school enquiry services into an education welfare service [25].

Commenting in a social work journal, Lady Plowden, chairman of the Committee on Children and their Primary Schools, put forward a personal view that the boundaries between the social service and education departments had been incorrectly drawn. 'It is disturbing', she argued, 'to find the suggestions that day nurseries should be under the social services departments rather than under the education department . . . It is equally disturbing to find the suggestion that the training of nursery nurses and assistants should be the responsibility of the social service departments . . . The same lack of appreciation of the relationship between education and out-of-school activities comes in the Seebohm suggestion that area-teams of social workers should play a major part in the development of community schools'[26]. The Chief Education Officers gave their whole-hearted support to this view.

A commitment to Seebohm

From February 1969, Crossman was regularly asked in the Commons for a statement on the government's position but, apart from officially condemning reorganization by some local authorities in advance of Seebohm [27], he refused to be drawn. In June the long-awaited Royal Commission on Local Government produced its conclusions [28], and the following month the office of the Lord President of the Council

presented its memorandum on the issues arising from the Seebohm
Committee. At this point both Crossman and Callaghan felt able to
make specific statements about the committee's proposals but when at
last they did so their answers conflicted. Crossman stated, in a written
answer to a parliamentary question, that the government aimed to
conclude their consultations in the autumn and would announce their
decisions then [29]. On the same day, in an oral answer, Callaghan
maintained that he would like to make a statement within the following
month [30]. Although the cabinet discussed the matter, however, no
public statement was made before the summer recess. It had been
decided, nevertheless, that the Queen's speech should contain a commitment to legislate on some of the committee's proposals.

Discussion

The year following the publication of the Seebohm Committee's report
was an interesting and eventful one for, within that twelve-month
period, the Cabinet's position on the committee's major suggestions
changed totally from a complete rejection of the report to a general
commitment that its main conclusions would be implemented. At the
beginning of this chapter it was suggested that four factors taken
together largely explain the timing and shape of the Social Services
Act, 1970; the policies being planned in related fields, the strategies of
pressure groups, the influence of individuals and the general election
of 1970. The first three of these help to determine why there was no
immediate government commitment to the Seebohm proposals and
why such an undertaking was made a year later.

The Cabinet's initial hostility to the committee's report might have
been a more serious hurdle had it been necessary to make the final
policy decisions in July 1968. This was unnecessary, however, since it
could legitimately be argued that decisions on the future of the personal
social services would have to await those on the reorganization of the
health service and local government. The B.M.A.'s rejection of the
government's green paper on the National Health Service in February
1969 inevitably meant delays on all fronts. Only when the Maud report
was published in June and received a rapid acceptance by the government was a commitment on Seebohm forthcoming.

This delay gave pressure groups time to marshall their arguments and
develop their campaigns. Recognizing that there was little enthusiasm
for Seebohm within governmental circles the social workers were the
most active, forming themselves into a well-organized political pressure

group whilst the medical officers began to realize what they stood to lose and started, at this late stage, to defend their existing responsibilities. Meanwhile, the local authority associations kept silent, reserving their judgements until the Royal Commission on Local Government reported.

Crossman's indifference to the committee's proposal might have condemned the report to a dusty shelf had there been no vociferous groups and powerful individuals able to persuade him otherwise. The social work pressure groups were undoubtedly helped by the influence of the civil servants in the welfare divisions of the D.H.S.S. The latter were firmly of the opinion that the Seebohm proposals should be implemented. In turn, they were supported by Baroness Serota without whom, Crossman has argued, he would have remained unconvinced. Whilst the merits of the Seebohm Committee were debated, the medical divisions of the department were preoccupied with the reorganization of the health service. Hence, they had little time to oppose changes within local government which would undermine the medical officer of health's existing preserve.

By the summer parliamentary recess of 1969, the decision to implement parts of the committee's proposals had been taken but no decisions had been made on which parts these would be. According to Crossman, one aspect was certain: Callaghan and he had made a pact that, whilst Callaghan remained Home Secretary, none of the responsibility for the children's services would be transferred to the D.H.S.S.

6 Tipping the Scales
(August 1969 – May 1970)

The Queen's speech of October 1969 announced that legislation arising from the Seebohm recommendations and from fresh proposals on the future administration of the National Health Service would be introduced during that session [1]. Machinery to process plans for the health service was quite straightforward to arrange, a small planning unit being created within the Department of Health and Social Security to prepare the next green paper. As before, however, it was impossible to locate the final decision-making machinery for the personal social services in one department and consequently an interdepartmental planning group had to be established under the guidance of an Under Secretary in the Home Office. Both teams were limited in influence, being primarily concerned with the nuts and bolts of preparing a government statement in one case and with drafting legislation in the other. Meanwhile, most of the important political decisions still had to be made, and here the key ministers involved were Crossman and Baroness Serota at the Department of Health; Callaghan and Shirley Williams at the Home Office.

Pressure Groups: The End Game

Following the publication of the Maud Report, the main interest groups involved were asked to comment on the Seebohm Report in the light of the new proposals. This period is perhaps the most intriguing for those interested in pressure group activity because, for the first time, there was some attempt at communication between them and, secondly, because once it was clear that most of the Seebohm Committee's recommendations would be implemented the strategies of some groups changed.

The medical associations had continually demonstrated their general opposition to the ideas contained in the Seebohm Report but by the latter part of 1969 the views of the Society of Medical Officers of Health and the British Medical Association changed direction and became more specific. The opinion of both groups was similar, although their approach differed. If they could not prevent reorganization of the personal social services, they hoped at least to be able to salvage control of the socio-medical services within the existing health departments and particularly those relating to the mentally disordered.

The medical officers modified their tactics by producing for the Secretary of State a list of services ranking them in order of the priority they attached to retaining them within the health service. The top five in order of preference were services for the mentally disordered, child guidance, services for the elderly, rehabilitation of the physically handicapped and social work in schools [2]. In October some of them met Crossman to discuss their views which were underlined later in a formal letter from the secretary of the S.M.O.H. The medical officers seem to have been politically isolated at this stage, the only evidence of any co-operation between their society and other groups being contained in a letter from the Health Visitors' Association to Crossman expressing broad approval for the society's views.

Whereas the medical officers compromised by specifying the services they would least wish to lose, the British Medical Association tried another tactic. Its main line of defence had been to stress the confidentiality issue, a useful weapon since it provided a rationale for medical control of socio-medical services whilst appearing to put the clients' interests first. At this point the B.M.A. extended its argument and made its real objections more explicit. In a report sent to Crossman in June 1969 the association argued that 'The status of the medical profession has been built over centuries . . . The social worker is a comparatively new and welcome addition to the team. But the administrators and para-medical personnel can only be regarded as members of a team whose captaincy is not in question' [3].

The British Medical Association's position regarding the Seebohm proposals was modified in August and September. During the summer, the County Council's Association (C.C.A.) and the B.M.A. met several times to discuss whether an area of agreement could be found between them [4]. Together they decided that a step-by-step solution would be desirable. In the first instance, they argued, any legislation on Seebohm should include only children's and welfare services in the new social service department. For the time being the health services should be excluded since these were tied to the continuing consideration of the National Health Service. The C.C.A.'s position had changed little from its original evidence to the Seebohm Committee, but for the B.M.A. the compromise was significant. Ideally the latter wished to see changes in the personal social services await decisions on the health service and local government reform but, failing that, legislation which excluded the most sensitive boundary issues—those concerning care for the mentally disordered and child guidance services—would be acceptable. In October 1969 representatives of the two associations met with Crossman and senior civil servants from the Department of Health and Social Security and the Ministry of Housing and Local Government to discuss these suggestions.

Whilst the C.C.A. and B.M.A. could find common ground on the timing of reform, the local government associations disagreed with medical groups over the location of certain services. Since, by this time, it was clear that the existing local health services would be removed from the auspices of local government, they were understandably anxious to retain as many socio-medical services as possible within the social service departments and hence within local government. Both the C.C.A. and the Association of Municipal Corporations (A.M.C.) argued that social workers in the mental health field and home helps should come under the social service departments and that the child guidance services should be retained by the education department [5]. In addition to the issues of timing and boundaries, the question of control by central government was a major preoccupation for the local authority associations and on this they refused to compromise. They objected, as they had always done, to a statutory committee and chief officer whose appointment would be subject to ministerial control [6].

It was not until final decisions on the Bill to reorganize the personal social services were being taken that the medical profession at last began to show its teeth. The Society of Medical Officers of Health had opposed the Seebohm Committee's report from the beginning but its medical colleagues, and especially the B.M.A., were quite obviously preoccupied with the question of health service reorganization and only peripherally concerned with the issues raised by the committee. Once it became clear, however, that the social service departments were almost certain to be introduced, the association began to be more specific and forceful in its opposition, seeking alliances to strengthen its case and arguing strongly for the retention of certain socio-medical services under the control of doctors. It cannot have been easy to reach a compromise with the County Councils' Association since the local authority associations generally were not enamoured of the medical lobby which had rejected the inclusion of a new unified health service within a local authority framework.

Although social workers had no need to modify their position, once it was clear that legislation on some of the Seebohm Committee's proposals would be passed, they wished nevertheless to seek out possible areas of agreement with other interest groups. In August they contacted both the C.C.A. and A.M.C. but the attempt at co-operation was not very successful. The C.C.A. would only meet representatives of the Standing Conference of Organisation of Social Workers if the acknowledged purpose of the meeting was not specifically related to the Seebohm proposals [7]. A meeting was arranged with the A.M.C. but the latter would make few comments until planning on the health services was made known. The only point of agreement found was that both organizations disapproved of any efforts by local authorities to pre-empt reform of the personal social services. The conference files indicate that some members wished to contact the medical profession but they were somewhat at a loss to know how to initiate discussions without risking a rebuff. There is no evidence, however, that such an initiative was ever taken.

In October 1969 the chairman of the Standing Conference and three other social worker representatives met Crossman, Shirley Williams and several civil servants. Crossman put the view that it would be very difficult to implement Seebohm in advance of decisions on the reorganization of local government. The social workers were asked for the answers to three questions, which they provided in November after consideration by the full conference. Crossman wished to know their justification for the introduction of Seebohm legislation in advance of other, more general governmental reforms. The social workers replied that there was the danger of pre-empting on a large scale, and that the potential for improving the services under review was being further undermined by the movement of social workers to Scotland where new social work departments were already being formed. Moreover, they argued, local government reform could be facilitated by the existence of the regrouped departments. Social workers were also asked what they felt was the essential core of Seebohm, the implication being that only part of the package might be implemented in the first instance. The only services the conference excluded from the committee's list of suggested social service department responsibilities were the management of child guidance services and the school psychological service. It felt that all other services were essential. The third question asked was how to ensure that residential and day care services for the mentally disordered could be co-ordinated with hospital care for that group if the former services remained with the local authorities. The reply was that it was vital to retain management of these services within the departments which arrange admissions and discharges. A special grant-in-aid from the minister was suggested as a means of injecting additional resources into this neglected area.

It was clear to the representatives of the Standing Conference attending the meeting with Crossman that the medical organizations had made a very strong bid for residential and other care services for the mentally disordered. The same point was made very forcibly at a subsequent meeting between the social workers and ministers (excluding Crossman, who was ill) on 1 December. To underline the solidarity amongst social workers for the Seebohm proposals, the Association of Psychiatric Social Workers, one of the members of the conference, submitted a second round of evidence, emphasizing its view that day residential care for the psychiatrically disordered should be a responsibility of the social services department. It felt that these services should be rehabilitative and not merely an extension into the community of the protective aspects of hospital care. Moreover, it was argued that local authorities already had experience of these services and that services for this group required close integration with the community.

Having received assurances that legislation on Seebohm would proceed, the social workers were anxious to protect their gains against the medical protagonists. They could not present a united front on certain internal matters, notably the training arrangements, but where their interests were threatened most—on the question of services for the mentally disordered—their solidarity was remarkable.

Final Decisions

The experience of this study suggests that it is not difficult for a researcher to discover the major preoccupations, battlegrounds and allegiances of pressure groups but much more so to determine how important decisions were finally made within political and civil service circles. The key issues to be resolved in the last few months of 1969 were the intractable ones of central-local relationships, demarcation lines between agencies (and especially the location of certain mental health services), and social work training arrangements. Before discussing these, however, it is worth recording the absence of an issue which usually looms large in policy negotiations—that of finance.

Finance

It was deliberately decided[1] that the Bill to implement parts of the Seebohm Committee's recommendations would be, in the words of the Under Secretary primarily responsible for the drafting, 'purely a machinery bill laying a duty on local authorities to create one sort of officer rather than another'. Unlike the Social Work (Scotland) Act, the counterpart for England and Wales was to place no general duty to promote welfare upon the new social service departments and would include no cash-giving functions in addition to those provided for in existing statutes. This meant that there was no need for a financial resolution to be passed alongside the Bill and hence the complexity of negotiations and especially those with the Treasury could be reduced. Of course, this is not to say that there was no recognition of the fact that legislation would almost certainly lead to pressure from local authorities for increases in Exchequer aid, but this was expenditure which could be debated at a later date. The decision to simplify the Bill as much as possible was vital to its success. The Schedule for the legislation was so tight that even with a short and straightforward Bill, debates in the Lords had to be curtailed to pass the legislation before the general election in June 1970. The Bill would almost certainly have failed to get through if additional finance had been involved.

Central–local relationships

Determining the exact relationship between the central and local agencies required three key decisions: whether to create a statutory committee, whether there should be a statutory director of social services and whether to allow the Secretary of State the right of veto on chief officer appointments. We have already noted that the local government associations vigorously opposed such restrictions on local autonomy, yet the Bill included all three constraints. We can only speculate as to the reasons, since those involved were unwilling to be very specific about the rationale for their decisions. The most obvious reason is that policy-makers wished to minimize local variations between authorities. The previous structure had accommodated considerable differences and pre-empting by some local authorities before the implementation of Seebohm indicated that there could continue to be widespread variation if the structure was determined by local decisions. Moreover, if in

[1] It has been impossible to discover exactly when the decision was taken but it is most likely to have been discussed within the Cabinet when the future of the N.H.S. and personal social services was considered in July.

many areas health departments took over social service functions, the reorganization of the health services could cause much greater up-heavals than if the social service departments were uniform and separate. Although the local authority associations continued to protest at the controls included in the Bill even up to the committee stage they won no concessions.

Boundaries between agencies

The demarcation lines between the new departments had been con-stantly debated since the formation of the Seebohm Committee but by this stage the issue was limited largely to the mental health field. Since education and housing welfare services were not statutorily based there was no need to include provisions for these in the Bill. The transfer of the home help services and other social work functions of the health departments, such as aid to unsupported mothers, was not hotly contested by the medical profession and therefore it was not necessary to arbitrate between competing pressure groups. Similarly, the inclusion of all children's and welfare department services within the new agency was by this time uncontentious.

The location of the residential and day care provisions for the mentally disordered was an interesting issue. Crossman was preoccupied with the reorganization of the health services and spent considerable time discussing the demarcation lines between the new health and personal social services. The mental health issue was clearly very finely balanced and the scales could have tipped either way. Several of those involved have said that even as late as Christmas 1969 Crossman was in favour of placing these provisions within the health departments, yet the Bill allocated them to the social service departments.

In the view of the civil servants from the social work divisions of the Department of Health and Social Security,[1] the case for these services to be located within the Seebohm departments was strong. Essentially there were three main arguments. Recent evidence had shown that the medical care of the long-stay mentally handicapped left much to be desired. In March 1969 the report of an enquiry into Ely Hospital, Cardiff [8], had been published and the report had wide-reaching implications. The department's Annual Report for 1969 remarked

> From it has stemmed a complete reassessment of the services provided
> for the mentally handicapped in this country both in hospital and in the
> community and much time and thought is now being given, both in the

[1] They were supported in their views by Baroness Serota.

department and outside it, to considering ways in which these services
and hospital services for other long-stay patients can be improved [9].

One result of the enquiry was a greater emphasis within the department on community services for the mentally handicapped. The abuses
described weakened the case for medical control and hence improved
the case for including residential and day care for this group in the
social services departments.

The second argument was summarized by Baroness Serota in a
public lecture. 'The amalgamation of the medically orientated social
work services with the non-medically orientated social work services
helps to establish the principle of universality in those areas where
social work is still somewhat tainted with stigma' [10]. The third
strand in the social work case was that the basis for the demarcation of
the social services should be that of the grouping of the main skills
required to provide them. Whereas the Seebohm Committee had
stressed the administrative and resource rationale for the demarcation,
primary skill was not a criterion which was developed in any detail.
Unfortunately, however, when trying to reach decisions on the future
of the mental health services, broad administrative reasons such as the
reduction of divided responsibility, the need for more powerful departments to attract resources and the inadequacy of knowledge about
needs and provisions to meet needs were of little help. Using the
criterion of primary skill, however, the social workers could argue with
some justification that for most of the time social work rather than
medical skills was required.

It was by using the principle of primary skills that all the decisions
regarding the boundaries between the health and personal social
services were finally taken. Crossman explains his decision thus:

> I was aware that the ancillary services in the Health Service resented
> the domination of the doctors and were not very satisfied. I didn't want
> to transfer, therefore, from democratically-controlled local authority
> into an autocratic health service any social workers who wanted to stay
> with the local authority. Health centres was the one area which clearly
> belonged in the health service and should be transferred. About the rest
> I was prepared to draw a line which, if possible, roused the least fury
> among the doctors who wanted the whole thing. The decision how to
> draw the line was the one on which I took most time and trouble and
> that meant avoiding as far as possible being over-influenced by the work
> of the lobbies. In order to escape the lobbies I laid down the principle
> myself that the issue should be decided, as far as possible, by medical
> skills on one side of the line, social welfare skills on the other [11].

The second green paper on the National Health Service explains the principles behind the demarcation in similar vein.

After carefully considering the contrasting views expressed on these questions, the government has decided that the services should be organised according to the main skills required to provide them rather than by any categorisation of primary user. Any alternative would involve the establishment of more than one local service deploying the same skill . . . The scarce skills of professional people will be used to greatest advantage if those of each profession are marshalled and husbanded by one agency in each area. Moreover, it will more often be possible to provide for users the advantages of continuity of care by one professional worker of any one discipline. Classification by skill will also help to enhance professional standards [12].

Training

The third contentious issue which remained unresolved until the last minute was that of the training arrangements for social workers. This was an issue about which Baroness Serota felt strongly.[1] She had tried hard to persuade some members of the Seebohm Committee to support a training council financed at least in the first instance by the government and the committee had accepted her view. However, as we noted earlier, there was a strong current of social work opinion running in favour of a council independent of civil service influence and finally this view prevailed, probably largely because most organizations belonging to the Standing Conference believed in a greater degree of professional autonomy over training arrangements.

The Parliamentary Phase

The results of planning for the reorganization of the health service, the personal social services and local government were made public in February 1970 when the Local Authority Social Services Bill, the second green paper on the National Health Service and a white paper on Local Government Reform [13] were produced. Great emphasis had been placed on the co-ordination of these processes, but, ironically, the first of these documents was the only one to reach the statute book within the lifetime of that administration. Legislative changes in the structure of local government and the National Health Service had

[1] She had been a member of the Central Training Council in Child Care and was therefore accustomed to a council closely linked with the civil service.

been scheduled for the following parliamentary session. These, together with other important social legislation,[1] including Crossman's pension proposals on which legislation had been promised that session, had to be shelved. On 18 May it was announced that the dissolution of parliament would take place on 29 May.

The Bill which implemented many of the Seebohm Committee's proposals was non-contentious in a party-political sense. Although pressure groups lobbied M.P.s of all persuasions, there was little discernible difference in the official views of the parties. Of course, the opposition tried to make capital out of some aspects of the Bill, notably the lack of any commitment to confer responsibility for these services on one central department, the omission of a general duty on local authorities to promote welfare, the failure to guarantee further finance to these services and the mandatory nature of the proposals [14]. The overwhelming impression, however, was one of indifference—the debates were extremely poorly attended and they lacked the sparkle of more contentious legislation. It is well known that the social work services fire the imaginations of few M.P.s but, this apart, it has been suggested that another reason for the poor attendances may have been that time was short and room for manoeuvre consequently limited. The three planning processes mentioned above had all been extremely rushed leaving little room for finesse. Moreover, other Bills competed for attention in the race for completion before the election.[2] Despite the fact that the Bill was hurried through the Commons, amendments in the Lords had to be curtailed [15] so that the legislation could be finished in the last days of the parliamentary session. The Bill received Royal Assent on 29 May, the day parliament was dissolved.

In the legislation the social workers achieved much of what they fought for—statutory social service committees responsible for, amongst other services, day and residential provisions for the mentally disordered,[3] ministerial veto over the appointment of directors and an independent training council. They failed to secure one central govern-

---

[1] These included the Education Bill to enforce comprehensive secondary education, the Dangerous Drugs Bill and the Bill on Industrial Health and Safety.

[2] These included Alf Morris's private member's legislation, The Chronically Sick and Disabled Persons Bill, which also received Royal Assent on May 29th.

[3] Schedule One of the Act outlines the exact functions conferred upon these new committees; these included all those of the children's and welfare committees plus certain duties from the health, housing and education committees such as home helps, the care of expectant and nursing mothers, the care and after-care of the sick and the regulation of nurseries and child minders.

ment department in charge of the reorganized services,[1] the commitment
of additional finance or the transfer to the new agencies of social work
services which had developed in the housing and education departments.[2] Both the medical organizations and the local government
groups had good cause to regard this legislation as contrary to their
interests in some respects; the former because the local health departments were weakened as a result and the latter because considerable
central control over local government decisions was imposed.

Discussion

The major policy decisions on the reorganization of the personal social
services were taken at a time when it was known that a general election
could not be many months away. In the final stages of the planning
process the most important influences were the last-ditch attempts by
pressure groups to modify the legislation, the interplay of key policy-
makers and the shadow of an impending election.

The knowledge that a general election was in the offing encouraged
the policy-makers to work quickly. The government had promised to
include this reorganization in its programme for the parliamentary
year. Indeed, it was one of the few parts of the Labour government's
social programme which had reached the stage where a Bill could be
drafted. By paring the legislation down to the bare minimum and
curtailing the parliamentary process, it was possible to obtain Royal
Assent just before the election. Had the policy been more technically
complicated, more expensive or more politically contentious it would
almost certainly have met the fate of the Labour government's plans
for pensions, local government reform and health service reorganization.

In the final stages of the policy's formulation the most important
pressure groups jockeyed for positions, modifying their demands and
forming new alliances where expediency dictated. The social work
activists were, however, very successful in their fight to preserve a
large part of the Seebohm package for legislation. As important as the
outcome of this campaign for the future of the social work profession
was the fact that between 1968 and 1970 this group became a coherent
political force for the first time, forging much closer links with civil
servants than had previously been possible. There were some issues,

[1] The Department of Health and Social Security was given this responsibility
very soon after a Conservative government was returned to office in June 1970.
[2] These could, however, be transferred later without the passing of any
specific legislation.

internal to social work, on which they failed to reach agreement but they demonstrated most effectively that they could achieve solidarity over the really contentious questions. Deep divisions in social work opinion which have developed since then suggest that this degree of cohesion was probably extremely difficult to achieve. It is worth adding that whilst this group could do little to affect the timing of reform, their efforts with respect to questions of training were influential. Here the majority view presented by social work organizations prevailed despite the fact that Baroness Serota, whose advice on other issues was decisive, favoured the opposite solution.

It would be wrong to see the clash of interests over Seebohm as involving a straight fight between the medical profession and social workers. The former were competing with one hand tied behind their backs in the sense that for most doctors the Seebohm proposals were of little significance in comparison with the issues confronting them over the reorganization of the health service. Only the local government medical officers saw their future significantly threatened by a reshuffle of the personal social services. Once it was realized that the Seebohm suggestions might threaten the community health teams which were developing as part of the health services, the B.M.A. began to defend their competence to retain certain services and successfully enlisted the support of the County Councils' Association for a compromise proposal but their campaign began too late to be really effective.

The position of the local authority associations—the third major group involved at this stage—was complicated. Their primary concerns were to defend local autonomy and to protect local government against the depletion of its services. They put their weight behind the doctors over the timing issue and behind the social workers on the question of the location of the community mental health services. In common with the medical profession, however, the local authority associations were preoccupied. Much more important, for them, were the impending changes in local government structures.

Finally, the interplay of political and civil service opinion within the Department of Health and Social Security was clearly important in determining the eventual shape of the legislation. We noted earlier that Crossman had to be persuaded that *any* reorganization of the personal social services was necessary at that time. His interest in, amongst other policies, the reform of the health service had always taken precedence over consideration of social work issues. This meant that when the boundary between the two services had to be drawn, Crossman's initial preference was to allocate the services in which there was both

a medical and a social component to the health service. The fact that
he was persuaded to change his mind was the final triumph of the
pro-Seebohm lobby both inside and outside Crossman's department
but it was the former group who achieved it. Only weeks before the
Bill was published the civil servants in the social welfare divisions of
the department, powerfully supported by Baroness Serota, managed to
convince Crossman that, using the principle of 'primary skill', social
services for the mentally disordered should be a social service department responsibility.

7 Policy Development

Two general themes underly the preceding chapters. The relative brevity and simplicity of the Social Services Act, 1970, disguised years of complicated decision-making on the part of many diverse individuals and groups. The delineation of boundaries around the organizations which deliver our social welfare services is no easy technical exercise. It involves recognition that any re-definition will bring new problems, whatever the criterion or combination of criteria used. It involves making important assumptions about the scale of state provision and the groups to which this will be directed. In this country it involves decisions on the relationship between welfare services and other social services, such as education, health, housing and social security. It involves recognizing that the nature and effectiveness of the service delivery system is vital in determining the outcomes of broad policy decisions on levels of expenditure, the social needs to be met and so on. It necessitates an intimate knowledge of the manpower resources available to provide social services and an awareness of their problems.

Secondly, policy changes within the personal social services which took place in 1970 were not ones which could have been predicted with certainty five years earlier. The conflicts between individuals, interest groups and departments were such that it is perhaps surprising that any changes took place at all. This final chapter looks first at the policy developments under review in the preceding chapters, singling out for discussion some of the more striking features of this particular case study. It is important, however, for those interested in policy analysis, that researchers immersed in the detail of their own studies do not neglect the wider questions of how their findings relate to other policy developments and whether the priority accorded to their policies can perhaps be explained by more general propositions. It is to these considerations that we turn in the second part of the chapter.

The Birth of the Social Services Departments

The starting point for this study was a brief examination of the expansion of local authority welfare services since 1948 and changes in their character; the legislative framework on which these services were built, and the pressures which arose from the structural decisions taken in the immediate post-war period. Health and welfare services were made the responsibility of the Ministry of Health, whereas services for deprived children were put in the hands of the Home Office. The result was that planning for these services took place *within* two separate ministries rather than *between* them, and, consequently, a comprehensive examination of the social work services was not possible for almost twenty years. Rivalries at central government level were paralleled by similar divisions between local government departments. These were exacerbated by the greater care devoted to planning the services for children in comparison with those for the elderly and handicapped during the nineteen-forties. Child care services from the outset, had certain advantages denied to health and welfare. Children's departments undoubtedly benefited from the simplicity of their administrative structure, prescribed by statute; health and welfare services were subject to great variations in structure and responsibilities, depending upon the whim of each local authority (subject to ministerial approval). The post-war children's services could build upon an explicit and coherent charter for a major sector of its work; health and welfare services were in large measure merely a reshuffling of existing responsibilities with no clear rationale. Thus, whilst every county and county borough had a children's department, health and welfare services might be the responsibility of a separate health and welfare committee, a combined health and welfare committee, a health committee with responsibility for welfare functions, or, indeed, some of them might be delegated to a lower-tier authority altogether.

From its first days, this structure had its critics but most early commentators took the view that co-ordination, as opposed to major structural changes, was the way to improve the range and quality of services. A similar trend can be seen in the criticisms of the tripartite structure of the health service created in 1948, when the delivery of health care was divided into the hospitals, general practice and local authority services. The early pressures for change stressed strengthening the links between existing agencies rather than a radical reorganization. This focus on improved co-ordination can be seen as arising in part from a genuine belief that minor alterations to the existing system can effect great improvement and, in part, from the knowledge that it is politically difficult to achieve major structural upheavals very frequently. Once a large-scale reorganization has been undertaken within any area of government—or indeed outside—there are many obvious pressures to make the best of what results in the short run rather than to repeat the traumas of radical change.

The extent to which the children's services became divorced from welfare services for other groups was underlined for me by the accounts by individuals from different service backgrounds of the important events which culminated in the creation of the Seebohm Committee. Those who had been involved in the administration and delivery of the children's services tended to stress the growth of ideas concerning a family service and the importance of concern over levels of juvenile crime. Those involved with various aspects of the health and welfare services focused upon the emergence of the community care approach and the gradual acceptance of a greater generic element in the training of social workers. The relative importance of these trends is impossible to pin down precisely but it is clear that in both welfare services there were pressing, though sometimes different, reasons for wanting a reappraisal of the structure.

In addition to the structural barriers which existed throughout the fifties and sixties, there were embryonic attempts to draw social workers of different types together through universal associations, by developing some common training element and through attempts, especially during the early fifties, to limit access to the 'profession'. These were, however, only preliminary steps. Success in achieving a feeling of unity had to await the knowledge that a departmental base from which to practise as a profession, with a status similar to that of education or health departments, was more than a remote possibility.

By the mid-sixties social work was practised in two major local authority departments, the welfare and children's departments, and as adjuncts to three others, health, education and housing. The structure had been in existence for almost twenty years during which time pressure for change had slowly grown. There were good reasons internal to the social services for justifying a reappraisal but social policy in general is of low priority in the wider political context. Whilst relatively unimportant generally, however, a few aspects of social policy are deemed by politicians to be important; in particular those relating to social control. We noted earlier that there was disagreement in the extent to which those involved in the process saw rising crime rates as a basic source of pressure for change but there was concensus that, as an issue, this and the levels of juvenile crime provided a catalyst, a basis upon which wider social reforms could be justified. In a pre-electoral period it carried sufficient weight to warrant special consideration by a Labour Party committee and the promise of action by a future Labour government.

Reactions against the idea of a family service as advocated by the Longford Committee, and later by Douglas Houghton and Home Office planners, came from a small and select group. They were politically somewhat diverse but had an interest and an eminence within the social services network in common. Their influence was essentially personal, and their request for a committee of enquiry was fed straight into political circles through contacts with key ministers. These pressures brought about a dual reaction—support from some and fierce opposition from a few of those who had nurtured the concept of a family service. Given this opposition, the small pressure group were lucky to succeed but the enquiry was only won at some cost; the terms of reference were limited in important respects, the membership was carefully balanced in terms of departmental support, and (un-successful) attempts were made in the early stages to influence the committee by attempts to limit the time it could take to report.

Any committee of enquiry will have a mixture of functions, and opinions will vary as to the exact part it should play in the planning process [1]. The Seebohm Committee was no exception. The value placed upon its eventual contribution depended upon the various expectations of those involved. Those who saw the committee as an advisory body established to produce a rapid synthesis of members' views were dismayed by the breadth of opinion canvassed and the time the committee took to present its findings. Those who viewed the enquiry as an opportunity for generating evaluative research on the existing services were disappointed in that, although the committee drew an impressive picture of the welfare provision available in the mid-sixties, no evaluative work of use in making policy decisions was forthcoming. Those who hoped that the committee would approach its task by defining a clear set of goals and designing a service in accord-ance with these were again disappointed. The committee's approach was incremental, their definition of the problem to be solved being entirely in terms of the deficiencies of, and marginal improvements to, the existing system.

A well-established function of enquiries is to 'educate public and group opinion, both through their reports and through the continuing dialogue that takes place while they are deliberating' [2]. The Seebohm

Committee did this supremely well, considering a vast amount of written and oral evidence and extending its educative functions even beyond the production of the report by arranging for members to explain their recommendations to a large number of groups up and down the country. A recent publication has implied that the educative role is usually subordinate to other more important ones [3]. In this case most observers to whom I talked saw the primary function of the Seebohm Committee as facilitating an examination of a range of services which spanned existing departmental boundaries, since past experience suggested that interdepartmental planning in this field was probably impossible to achieve.

The committee defined the basic problems it faced very early in its proceedings, even before evidence was sought. This definition narrowed considerably the range of solutions open to it and thus limited the influence of evidence on the broad organizational framework suggested. The evidence was more useful to the committee when more specific issues were being considered, such as the exact boundaries, central-local relationships, specialization and training.

Whilst the committee was sitting, a very wide variety of pressure groups was involved, ranging from the large, well-run professional, bodies to small voluntary organizations, and interest groups formed specially to give evidence to the committee. The membership of the committee, although balanced in terms of departmental allegiances, contained a sizeable majority with social work interests, two specifically included for their local government background and only one with medical expertise. This imbalance in the sectional interests represented resulted in fewer battles over the relationship between the medical profession and social workers than over the extent of central government influence on the reorganized services, the issue of central control being hotly contested by the local government members. Many of the less important disputes are disguised in the report by careful phraseology, and basic disagreements between members are described diplomatically in the body of the report rather than in notes of dissent at the end.

To those interested in the services under review the analysis and conclusions of the Seebohm Report came as little surprise. This was due partly to the fact that the committee took so long to report and opinions had modified during that period. The unstartling nature of the findings suggests that the committee's function as an educator had already been successful. It was also partly due to the fact that the main conclusions had been leaked to the press three months before the publication of the report.

R.T.W.—5

In July 1968, the planning of the personal social services was placed firmly back in the political arena where the Seebohm proposals competed with other important social policy developments for the attentions of the key ministers and particularly of Richard Crossman, then Secretary of State for the Social Services. He made it quite clear that his interests lay in the planning of his pension scheme and the future of the health services rather than in the personal social services. He was only interested in the latter when they raised issues which impinged upon the health service. This meant that on many of the report's suggestions he was willing to be influenced by the civil servants in the social work divisions of his department and in particular by Baroness Serota, who as a member of the Seebohm Committee was well acquainted with, and committed to, most of its recommendations.

The pressure group activity at this stage had distilled into an interprofessional dispute between the social workers and doctors, with local government representatives intervening to fight for local autonomy but supporting both of the other protagonists on different issues. The post-report period was characterized by a particularly fierce and effective campaign by social work activists who feared that apathy in political circles and opposition from the medical profession and some individual local authorities, who were reorganizing services along anti-Seebohm lines, might destroy their chances of success. Contrasting markedly with this approach were the tactics of the medical profession, who were understandably preoccupied with reorganization of the National Health Service, and who realized too late the dangers to parts of their empire which a Seebohm-type reform represented. Once they chose to defend their interests, and particularly the services for the mentally disordered, however, they very nearly succeeded in retaining their formal responsibility for socio-medical provisions for this group.

Social Policy Change

It is impossible to generalize from one case study about the factors which affect the fortunes of all social policies and which determine the priority accorded to them at any one time. No single case study can form the basis for this type of generalization. Nevertheless, by comparing a number of policy developments, it is perhaps possible to formulate propositions about the factors determining the priority attached to a particular issue. Such an exercise was attempted in a recent publication by myself and others in the hope that by testing our very tentative propositions against further studies it might be possible to improve, extend and refine these ideas [4]. This case study was not devised primarily with that aim in mind, but as it progressed it became clear that a number of these propositions were useful in explaining the predominance of some policy options over others.

Change, Choice and Conflict identifies three types of policy: those which involve totally new areas of state intervention (innovation), those which constitute an expansion of programmes already in operation (development), and those which entail a re-shaping of existing commitments in different forms (reform) [5]. Comparing six policy developments, two of each type, the above study concluded that there were possibly important variations in the factors governing the priority accorded to them. The introduction of the social services departments involved the recasting of existing services in a new mould; services which had developed piecemeal over many years were given a new unified structure within which to operate. Hence the policy was clearly a reformatory one and, as such, the decision-making process centred around certain sorts of arguments. We will return to these later.

Using the notion of a 'queue' of demands upon government, varying from the very specific to the very general, all competing for scarce resources of various kinds, the study suggests a number of factors which might affect the movement of such demands up and down the 'queue'. Firstly, there are 'general criteria' against which the merits of all issues are assessed. It is argued that issues which attain high levels of *legitimacy feasibility* and *support* usually do best and vice versa. Secondly, there are 'particular attributes' of the issues themselves which more precisely locate their position in the queue, helping to answer such questions as 'What features of an issue enhance its legitimacy?' and 'What is it about an issue which increases its support or decreases its feasibility?'

According to *Change, Choice and Conflict* a major hurdle which any prospective policy must clear is that of legitimacy [6]. This is determined by asking the question 'Is this an issue with which government considers it should be concerned?' The answer will depend upon current assumptions made about the appropriate role and sphere of government action and it is likely to vary with the ideology of the party in power and with its assessment of what 'public opinion' or important interest groups consider to be the legitimate boundaries of state intervention. Clearly, for every successful issue the answer to this question must be in the affirmative but *Change, Choice and Conflict* suggests that policies which constitute an innovation are more likely to involve lengthy debates about the legitimacy of state involvement than the other two types, since in the latter cases questions about changing

the boundaries of state responsibility will already have been answered
and will often be taken as given. In other words, the introduction of a
new scheme or, much more rarely, the total abolition of an existing one
will inevitably entail discussions about the limits of government
responsibility whereas the modification of existing programmes may
not. This study would seem to bear this out in that the legitimacy of
state provision in the services under review is taken as given, the
controversies centring not upon *whether* such services should exist at all
but in what form they should be organized and presented.

A second criterion upon which any successful issue must score at least
moderately well is that of feasibility [7]. The chances of an issue being
considered at all will depend upon our current state of knowledge and
technological sophistication. Thereafter, the process of determining
the feasibility of policy options can be a complex, often time-consuming
exercise. Some, like the reform of our pensions system, take so long
that successive governments have had difficulty in planning their proposals and implementing them within a single term of office. The more
options under consideration, the more complex the procedure can
become. The possible questions are almost endless. What will be the
costs, how far can these be predicted and who will bear them? How far
will extensions or modifications to existing capital equipment be
necessary? How many additional staff will be needed and what skills will
they require? Will new patterns of professional co-operation be necessary and how difficult will it be to achieve this co-operation? Does
adequate administrative capacity exist? Obviously the questions vary
from issue to issue. Not all questions will be asked of all policies and the
eventual selection of one solution rather than another may well depend
largely upon the limits within which feasibility is assessed. Inevitably,
however, the questions asked and the answers to them will depend upon
the predispositions, ideology and interests of those making the assessment.

In this case study considerations of feasibility were left very largely
to the central departments involved and in practice primarily to the
Ministry of Health. The Seebohm Committee spent very little time
considering the resource implications of its proposals; for example, they
did not attempt to estimate the extent of the increase in demand, the
overall cost of the reorganized services, the capital equipment necessary
and the additional manpower requirements. Indeed, we have seen that
it made a conscious decision to leave such an assessment very vague.
Subsequent assessments of feasibility by the responsible government
departments resulted in the implementation of the policy but only in a

limited form. Unlike other social policies being considered at the same time, the reforms proposed by the committee could be reduced to one fairly simple technical exercise with no financial implications and the Bill could be passed relatively quickly through parliament. In its limited form, this policy had additional advantages for the government in that, regardless of increases in demand, costs could be controlled by the Treasury, no immediate increase in manpower was absolutely necessary and it fitted in with other social policies being planned at the time; namely changes in the National Health Service structure and local government reform. Hence, the weaknesses of the Seebohm package— its vulnerability to dilution—proved also to be its strength; for it is reasonable to suppose that if the Bill had missed the election deadline, the social services departments might never have come into existence.

Issues may pass the tests of legitimacy and feasibility with flying colours and still founder. One reason for this may be that their 'support' rating is low. Policy-makers are continually making difficult predictions about the effects upon their credibility of certain courses of action. *Change, Choice and Conflict* maintains that because policy change redistributes, or is presumed to redistribute, an existing allocation of resources, whether they be income, power, influence or status, inevitably it will create some satisfaction and some discontent [8]. 'In almost all circumstances government finds itself in a position in which its actions have mixed consequences for support. There are some potential gains and some losses: trade-offs are assessed and the effects of cancelling out taken into account' [9]. The study distinguishes between the impact of policy changes upon both 'diffuse' and 'specific' support, the former relating to the general stock or standing of the government of the day within the country and the latter to the views of key interest and pressure groups within our political system. The introduction of certain policies may be thought to enhance the overall popularity of the government whilst at the same time seriously damaging its relations with important interest groups. Conversely, issues assumed to be generally contentious may be considered because they will find favour with certain key sections of the population.

In this case study assessments of both the diffuse and the specific support implications of various proposals were of very great importance. The reorganization of the personal social services involved some redistribution of power and status among a number of professional groups and therefore calculations of the specific support and opposition to various options were crucial. We have already noted the Seebohm Committee's valuable role in assessing, synthesizing and changing opinions on possible developments within the personal social services. Whilst the committee was, in Crossman's view, unconvincing in its demonstration of the feasibility of its proposals, it was much more successful at showing that support would be forthcoming from the social work groups involved. Subsequently, as we have seen, these groups themselves made clear their almost unanimous agreement as to the solutions they wished to see implemented. It was clear too, that the medical officers of health had much to lose but the social workers' support was not matched by equally strong opposition from the doctors. The medical profession were, on the whole, much less vociferous and many of them were content to accept changes in the personal social services if these were accompanied by reforms within the National Health Service. Hence, when balancing the reactions of the professional groups involved, it seemed likely in 1969 that the social workers would produce greater disruption to the existing services if the social services departments were rejected than would the medical officers if the dual reorganization took place.

Calculations concerning the effect upon diffuse support for the government were perhaps as important in explaining the introduction of the social services departments as the specific opinions of the pressure groups. Whilst the fortunes of the personal social services are not usually seen by policy-makers as of permanent and consuming interest to the general public, the advent of an election may modify this assessment. The failure of several important Labour government proposals to reach the statute books immediately prior to the general election of 1970 meant that the government were especially concerned to pass a politically uncontentious piece of social legislation before parliament was dissolved. Thus, whilst the issues themselves may not have attracted greater public interest during this period, their symbolic value was enhanced.

Following a difficult political reception, the Seebohm Committee's proposals eventually received acceptably high scores on the legitimacy, feasibility and support criteria but these alone do not fully explain the eventual implementation of the social services departments. Two 'specific attributes' of the issue, the 'origins' and the 'association and scope' have to be taken into account. *Change, Choice and Conflict* argues that the origins of an issue can affect the fortunes of a policy [10]. If an idea is promoted by an individual or group close to government (including the civil service), its chances of fairly rapid implementation are likely to be better than those of a proposal advocated from outside. 'We do not contend that only issues originating in or close to government gain priority, for this is patently not so. Issues of keen interest and concern to a minister can be blocked or diverted by his cabinet colleagues and pressure groups do win victories. But *prima facie* the closer to government the point of origin the better the prospects' [11].

The 'independent' committee which pushed the idea of social services departments into the political arena for the first time clearly operated from outside government. As an interdepartmental enquiry it was perhaps more isolated than committees established by one department. However, the appointment of an ex-member of the committee to a powerful political position strengthened the chances of implementation considerably and transformed the policy's origins from a possible disadvantage to a positive advantage.

The association of one issue with another or the deliberate detachment of one policy proposal from another may influence a policy's chance of success [12]. *Change, Choice and Conflict* suggests that policies developed from a position of weakness may be strengthened by careful association with policies which seem to have greater momentum. Alternatively, some policies may have greater chances of success if a deliberate strategy of isolation is pursued and the scope of the debate limited. In this case study one can see attempts at both association and disassociation. Efforts were made in the early sixties to widen the scope of the debate about juvenile delinquency. The momentum for change which had built up around the children's departments and their extension into a family service was harnessed in order to achieve a more comprehensive review of the social welfare services. Once such a review had been undertaken and the reorganization of the personal social services was placed firmly in the 'queue' of issues competing for government attention, its advocates then fought to isolate the policy. Their reasons for disassociation were that, if the introduction of the social services departments had to await the reorganization of local government and the National Health Service, it might never be implemented at all.

Postscript

The Local Authority Social Services Act, 1970, created social services departments, bringing together under one local authority committee and one department all the functions of the former children's and welfare departments and some services formerly provided by local authority health departments. In England and Wales the responsible authorities were the county and county borough councils, the London boroughs and the City of London, each of which had a statutory duty to create a social services committee and appoint a director of social services. In 1974, local government in England and Wales was completely reorganized, and the responsible authorities for social services outside London became the new non-metropolitan counties and metropolitan district councils.

Since 1971 when social services departments first came into operation, the scale of their activities has grown enormously. The average annual growth rate in personal social service expenditure (at constant 1970 prices) between 1968 and 1973 was 17.4% compared with an average of 3.2% for public expenditure as a whole [1]. Between 1969/70 and 1973/4 capital expenditure on the personal social services increased by £63 million (125% at 1974 survey prices) and current expenditure by £169.9 million (58%). In all, this accounts for a growth of 68% in five years [2].

If one considers staffing, here too the expansion of numbers has been striking. Table 2 (on page 123) indicates the extent of the increase and it is perhaps interesting that by far the largest percentage increase has occurred amongst welfare assistants.

As one would expect with an increase in the expenditure and manpower in the personal social services, the scale of activities has also expanded. Table 3 (on page 123) shows that there were substantial increases in the numbers of beneficiaries of selective services between 1970 and 1974.

Table 2   Manpower in Social Services Departments, 1972–4

England

	1972	1974	% increase, 1972–4
Management and supervisory staff	3,207	4,637	44·6
Social workers	9,328	12,760	36·8
Social work (welfare) assistants	1,118	2,578	130·6
Trainees	1,428	1,704	19·3
Home help organizers	1,197	1,578	31·8
Home helps	35,185	40,810	16·0

Derived from D.H.S.S. feedback statistics, 1973, 1975.

Table 3   Numbers of Beneficiaries of Selected Services: England and Wales

	1970	1974	Percentage growth, 1970–4 %
ELDERLY			
Residents in:			
(a) local authority homes	88,800	96,000	+ 8·3
(b) joint user premises (with health)	3,700	2,000	−45·9
(c) voluntary or private homes on behalf of local authorities	13,100	15,200	+16·0
Receiving home help	396,000	513,500	+29·7
Home help cases per 1,000 population over 65	62·3	76·0	+22·0
Meals provided:[1]			
(a) at home	15,000,000	19,200,000[2]	+28·0
(b) in clubs, centres	7,700,000	10,800,000[2]	+40·3
CHILDREN			
(a) in residential accommodation[3]	38,300	40,600[2]	+ 6·0
(b) with foster parents	30,300	29,800[2]	− 1·3
(c) in day nurseries	22,226	25,908	+16·6
MENTALLY HANDICAPPED			
(a) adult training centre places	22,857	33,575	+46·9
(b) home and hostel places	5,013	6,710	+33·9
MENTALLY ILL			
(a) workshop and day centre places	2,736	3,562	+30·2
(b) home and hostel places	1,900	2,432	+28·0

Source: R. Klein (ed.), op. cit., Table 3.3, p. 62.

Data provided by D.H.S.S. (Statistics and Research Division 6) and from Home Office, *Statistics relating to approved schools, remand homes and attendance centres in England and Wales for the year 1970*, Cmnd. 4879.

Notes: 1. Mainly to elderly but some to younger physically handicapped.
2. Figures for 1973.
3. Includes figures for approved schools and remand home places.

The period since reorganization has not been easy for the personal social services. In their early years social services departments have had to face many pressures, some emanating from within and others arising as a result of the general social difficulties of the time. In some ways the social, economic and political context within which these services are organized has changed considerably over the past few years but it is striking that many of the issues considered by the Seebohm Committee and later debated when framing the legislation have proved to be far from transient. They are not issues peculiar to the social services of the mid-sixties but perennial difficulties some of which have surfaced again within five years of reorganization. The problems facing the social services departments are numerous, but some of the more important ones are discussed below.

Double reorganization

As we have already seen, social services departments were formed in 1971 and underwent a second restructuring in 1974. The first reorganization produced the usual teething problems with administrative and field staff struggling to adjust to a larger organization, but these early years were not ones in which much valuable planning could take place since a second major upheaval was clearly almost inevitable. Not surprisingly, there were few complaints about the dual reform from social workers since most of them had fought for the early introduction of social services departments. Nevertheless, this prolonged period of uncertainty brought with it enormous problems of planning and service delivery.

Before 1971 there were 173 children's departments and 204 welfare authorities in England and Wales. Each had its own chief officer, professional and administrative staff. In the first reorganization, 174 social services departments were created and, in consequence, the number of chief officer appointments was reduced considerably. The second reorganization diminished the number of departments still further to 116, creating even larger organizations, taller hierarchies and fewer appointments at the most senior levels. A great many senior personnel in social services departments were displaced; some retired, some left the services and many were, in effect, demoted. It seems to be a feature of large-scale mergers that officials, particularly senior officials, are rarely completely displaced. The 1974 reorganization was no exception for personal social services departments. Posts were found for most of the senior officials with the result that many of the departments now seem rather top-heavy.

One further difficulty associated with such rapid change was the need for all the new agencies created by local government and health service reform to establish fresh relationships with each other.

Expanded statutory duties

Problems of reorganization were accompanied by an extension of the statutory duties placed upon social services departments. In particular, four statutes generated a great deal of extra work for the staff. The Children and Young Persons Act, 1969, removed the power of magistrates to allocate children directly to approved schools and remand homes and replaced this by a power to place children in the care of local authorities. Moreover, the latter were given responsibility for accommodating young offenders, a responsibility previously carried out by central government. The Act became a considerable embarrassment to social services departments which have neither the staff to care adequately for the numbers of children allocated to them nor the residential accommodation necessary. The Health Services and Public Health Act, 1968, placed a duty upon local authorities to provide a home help service which was adequate for the needs of the area, and included a new power to promote the welfare of the elderly. The Chronically Sick and Disabled Persons Act, 1970, placed several duties upon the new departments, one of which was to discover the number of disabled people within their province, to advertise their services and to provide such people with practical help and aids where necessary. The fourth statute to increase the burden upon social services departments was the National Health Service Reorganisation Act, 1973. The Act brought hospital social workers under the umbrella of the new department and placed a statutory duty upon the local authorities to co-operate with the health authorities in order to improve the health and welfare of people requiring both services.

Increased demand

Several factors have combined to increase the demand made upon social services departments in recent years. The 'one door' policy of the Seebohm Committee has led to greater ease of access to the services and the publicity surrounding reorganization, coupled with welfare rights campaigns, have improved clients' knowledge of the services available to them. Demographic trends exacerbate the problem in that the proportion of the dependant sectors of the population is rising. Added to this is the fact that in a period of economic recession the incidence of personal and family difficulty is likely to increase and hence new demands will be made upon social services departments. Many departments have come to look upon themselves as the 'dustbin' of the local authority; as social problems such as unemployment and homelessness increase, a greater number of families are placed at risk and hence become the potential clients of the social services department.

Financial limitations

For the first few years of the reorganization, expenditure on the personal social services grew at an unprecedented rate and planning took place on the basis that such an expansion would continue. Promises were made and new programmes scheduled. These must now be curtailed in the light of the grave economic situation and cut-backs in local authority expenditure. It is evident that social services departments have found it extremely difficult, not to say impossible, to make the necessary economies in the past year. In July 1974 the Secretary of State for the Environment warned them that they might have to plan for nil growth in revenue expenditure for 1975/6. The more optimistic planning of the past few years has presented considerable difficulties: for example some authorities have been unable to open newly built homes because they are unable to provide the staffing necessary. The need to make uncomfortable decisions about cuts in services and the consequent drastic reductions in some areas of their work will mean that the variations in local provision are likely to increase. Sadly, few senior staff have the requisite planning skills to undertake such complicated and difficult pruning exercises as may be required in the next few years. This raises questions as to whether the D.H.S.S. will find it necessary to increase their influence over decisions made at the local level. They may, for instance, consider it necessary to develop specific grants for certain projects in order to ensure that the variation in local provision is not too great. Such a move would, however, bring considerable difficulties since it would represent a significant change in direction regarding local government finance.

Manpower problems

Financial difficulties in the personal social services have been exacerbated by the fact that roughly two-thirds of expenditure on these services is devoted to staffing. In the past few years the problems of manpower have become particularly acute; with reorganization many of the more experienced field workers have moved up the hierarchy leaving a dearth of qualified staff at the local level. Despite post-Seebohm expansions in social work training programmes, still only about 39% of basic grade social workers have a recognized social work qualification and this leaves a high proportion of inexperienced and unqualified staff at the coal-face. Whatever the training deficiencies of social work field staff, however, the proportion of qualified workers in other parts of the local authority services is very much lower. This applies in particular to the residential services where on average only about 4% have professional social work qualifications, although in the residential child care field about 18% are professionally qualified. The lack of trained social work staff is causing great concern to the D.H.S.S. and to the Central Council for Education and Training in Social Work which was established to promote training in social work. A measure of this concern is the fact that despite the financial situation, a considerable expansion in training facilities for social work is planned in the next few years. The high cost of staffing raises the very sensitive subject of whether training for social work should take place at two levels; the continuation of existing qualifications in social work, plus a shorter, less intense training for para-professional staff. Such proposals are likely to be hotly contested by some existing qualified social workers.

Boundary difficulties

Inevitably the boundaries drawn with such difficulty around the social services departments have since caused some friction. That between the new health authorities and social services departments is a case in point. Any number of problems surround the relationship between health and social services, but two can be mentioned to illustrate the sort of difficulties and tensions which exist. First, some considerable resentment was caused by placing hospital social workers within the new social services departments rather than integrating them with the health authorities. Many doctors were suspicious of the closer contact thus established with the local authorities; medical social workers were concerned by the threat of separation from the hospital medical team.

The second illustration concerns the problems of implementing a community care policy for discharged hospital patients. The hospitals return their patients to the community and the local authority is responsible for their subsequent care. Health authorities complain that social services departments do not provide adequate community support services once a patient is discharged; social services criticize the hospitals for failing to notify them of people at risk. The local authority medical social workers are caught between the two. It is to be hoped that the newly created Joint Consultative Committees, consisting of health authority and local authority personnel, will iron out some of these difficulties.

The Seebohm Committee proposed that education welfare officers should be included in the new unified departments, but this has never been implemented on any large scale. Some local authorities have tried schemes which include the transfer of E.W.O.s to social services departments but these schemes have not met with great success. In future it is likely that the education welfare service will be encouraged to work closely with the social services department without being subsumed by it.

Another boundary which provides complications is that between the local authority department and the Supplementary Benefits Commission. The Seebohm Committee was in favour of making a firm distinction between the two, but this has proved very difficult in practice. Social workers have the power under the Children and Young Persons Act, 1963, to provide cash payments for families with children where they feel there is a need. This was intended originally to facilitate social workers undertaking preventive work with families, but it has since been used extensively to provide more general support for families in situations of financial difficulty. This use of 'Section I money' is resented by many social workers who feel that the Supplementary Benefits Commission should take full responsibility for clients' financial needs. It is only one of several reasons for there being considerable hostility between the two agencies at the local level.

Professional issues

The many problems faced by social services departments have clearly affected the morale of the professionals working within them. One frequently expressed concern is that the service now seems to be almost totally crisis-orientated with very little chance for preventive work. Myths have rapidly developed about how 'good' things actually were in the 'good old days' before reorganization when exactly the same criticism about the levels of crisis work were made of the child care and welfare services.

The specialist/generalist debate did not end with the introduction of the new departments. A major question today concerns the range of duties each worker should be tackling. This element of the Seebohm Committee's recommendations was perhaps the most misunderstood part of the report and the section most open to subsequent misquotation. The committee suggested that 'as a general rule, and as far as possible, a family or individual in need of social care should be served by a single social worker'. This was a plea that one social worker should take primary responsibility for each case, not that every social worker should be able to deal with any eventuality. The former interpretation (and indeed the committee's recommendation) allows for any amount of specialization amongst the field workers; the latter does not. Whilst the committee recommended that social workers should be able to take a wider view, it did not argue that all social workers should become totally 'generic' in their work. Many departments and directors of social services pursued genericism with great zeal and implemented the rapid integration of case loads. The low morale which for several years was a feature of the new departments must in part be attributed to the effects of the loss of specialist labels which, quite apart from the security they provide for the holders, are important as a source of status and prestige. To deny the importance of specialization—indeed to denigrate specialist knowledge as narrow and out of date—is to devalue the holder. Quite apart from the impact on the morale of the staff concerned, the move to the generic worker has also been blamed for a supposed loss of special skills for highly complicated tasks, such as working with disturbed adolescents. In this criticism the social workers themselves have been joined by other professional groups who have expressed concern about an apparent drop in standards. Whether or not these claims are justified, it is not surprising that many social service departments now seem to be moving explicitly in the direction of generic field work teams, containing specialist individuals and away from the model of the omnicompetent genericist.

Concern over the degree of specialization desirable in social work is accompanied by continual questioning and redefinition of the social worker's role in society. The pendulum swings back and forth on the question of whether social workers should concentrate on helping individuals and families to adjust to their circumstances or whether the onus should be upon attempts to change the society in which they live. How should these aims be achieved? As the latter view has gained currency in recent years, the social worker's relationship with the community and their involvement in community action has become an important issue. These concerns were in their infancy in the mid-sixties but the Seebohm Committee devoted a short chapter to the subject. It recommended that the new department should organize voluntary effort within the community and should promote public interest and involvement in the social affairs of the locality. The ways in which this could be done and the obvious pitfalls were not, however, spelt out and since 1970 discussions about conflicts facing community workers who are both public servants and local activists have become much more familiar.

The reorganization of 1970 brought with it radical changes in the professional bodies representing social workers. The British Association of Social Workers is much larger than any of the previous specialist social work groupings and its contacts with the civil service much stronger. Nevertheless, the remarkable degree of solidarity achieved by social workers when lobbying for the Local Authority Social Services Act has been eroded to some degree. Many younger social workers seem reluctant to join a professional body which they feel places the interests of the profession far higher than those of clients they are supposed to be helping. Others question the effectiveness of the association in influencing central government policy despite the better formal channels of communication. Perhaps most important, the association remains an exclusive club. Sixty per cent of all field workers in social services departments are debarred from full membership of the association because they are unqualified, and, despite a falling membership, existing members of the association voted in 1975 to perpetuate the embargo upon untrained staff.

Inevitably, the Seebohm reorganization left many of the basic problems of the personal social services unsolved; obtaining adequate resources for this sector, achieving co-operation between different professional groups and agencies, clarifying the role, if any, of the social worker in society. In the course of introducing the unified social services departments, certain problems were ignored and others were resolved only through compromise. It will be the difficulties arising from these weaknesses which will eventually form the rationale for a re-examination of the 'solutions' thought appropriate in the sixties.

Reference Notes

INTRODUCTION

1 *Report of The Committee on Local Authority and Allied Personal Social Services* (Seebohm Committee), Cmnd. 3703, July 1968.
2 Hall, P. K., Land, H., Parker, R. A., and Webb, A. L., *Change, Choice and Conflict in Social Policy*, Heinemann, 1975.
3 For a short discussion of the strengths and weaknesses of the case-study method *see* ibid., pp. 13–17.

CHAPTER ONE

1 *The Royal Commission on the Poor Laws and Relief of Distress* (Minority Report), 1905–9, Cmnd. 4499, p. 430 and *passim*.
2 ibid., Majority Report, p. 602.
3 ibid., Minority Report, pp. 422–3.
4 A brief discussion of the haphazard development of the health and welfare services before 1948 is given in Parker, J., *Local Health and Welfare Services*, Allen and Unwin, 1965, pp. 22–36.
5 For a stimulating account of developments in these services, see Packman, J., *The Child's Generation*, Blackwell, 1975.
6 The Home Department, Ministry of Health and Ministry of Education, *Report of the Care of the Children Committee* (Curtis Report), H.M.S.O., 1946, Cmnd. 6922.
7 National Assistance Act, 1948, Section XXI (i).
8 Parker, J., op. cit., p. 108.
9 Seebohm Report, op. cit., p. 276.
10 Central Statistical Office, *Social Trends*, No. 3, 1972, p. 59.
11 Goldman, Sir S., *Public Expenditure, Management and Control*, H.M.S.O., 1973, p. 69.
12 Examples of such reports are:
   Report of the Committee on Medical Auxiliaries (Cope Report), H.M.S.O., 1951, Cmnd. 8188.
   Report of the Committee on Social Workers in the Mental Health Services (Mackintosh Report), H.M.S.O., 1951, Cmnd. 8260.
   Report of the Committee on Maladjusted Children (Underwood Report), H.M.S.O., 1955.

Report of the Committee on Health Visiting (Jameson Report), H.M.S.O., 1956.

Report of the Committee on Social Workers in the Local Authority Health and Welfare Services (Younghusband Report), H.M.S.O., 1959.

Report of the Committee on Children and Young Persons (Ingleby Report), H.M.S.O., 1960, Cmnd. 1191.

13 The Younghusband Report defined social work as 'The process of helping people with the aid of appropriate social services, to resolve or mitigate a wide range of personal and social problems which they are unable to meet successfully without such help', op. cit., p. 3.

14 ibid., p. 123.

15 For a recent discussion see Jones, K., 'Better services for the mentally handicapped', in Jones, K. (ed.), *The Year Book of Social Policy in Britain, 1971*, Routledge and Kegan Paul, 1972, pp. 187–202.

16 *Report of the Royal Commission on Mental Illness and Mental Deficiency, 1954–57*, Cmnd. 169, p. 16.

17 Ministry of Health, *A Hospital Plan for England and Wales*, Jan. 1962, Cmnd. 1604, p. 9.

18 *Health and Welfare: the Development of Community Care*, H.M.S.O., 1963, Cmnd. 1973.

19 See the Younghusband Report, op. cit., p. 123.

20 For a brief discussion of key developments within social work, see McDougall, K., 'A Chairman's Eye View', *Social Work Today*, Vol. 1, No. 1, April 1970, p. 5, and *A.S.W. News*, April 1970, pp. ii–viii.

   A more detailed account is given in McDougall, K., 'B.A.S.W.: The British Association of Social Workers' in Jones, K. (ed.), *The Year Book of Social Policy, 1971*, Routledge and Kegan Paul, 1972, pp. 98–111.

21 See p. 47.

22 Jameson Report, op. cit., pp. ix–x.

23 Younghusband Report, op. cit., p. iv.

24 ibid., p. 3.

25 Home Office circular 157/50; Ministry of Health circular 78/50, Ministry of Education circular 225/50.

26 Donnison, D. V., *The Neglected Child and the Social Services*, Manchester University Press, 1954, p. 116.

27 Home Office circular 118/56; Ministry of Health circular 16/56; Ministry of Education circular 311/56.

28 *The Royal Commission on Local Government in Greater London 1957–1960*, October 1960, Cmnd. 1164, pp. 151–2.

29 Younghusband Report, op. cit., pp. 318–21.

30 Ingleby Report, op. cit., p. 16.

31 ibid., p. 19.

32 Donnison, D. V., Jay. P. and Stewart, M., *The Ingleby Report: three critical essays, Fabian Research Series* 231, Dec. 1962, p. 9.

33 Council for Children's Welfare, *A Family Service or a Family Court*, 1965.

34 Hastings, S. and Jay, P., *The Family and the Social Services*, Fabian Society, Feb. 1965.

CHAPTER TWO

1 *Crime: a Challenge to us All* (The Longford Report), Report of a Labour Party Study Group, June 1964.

2 The Longford Report, op. cit., p. 16.

3 ibid., p. 23.

4 ibid., p. 16.

5 Scottish Home and Health Department and Scottish Education Department, *Children and Young Persons in Scotland* (The Kilbrandon Report), April 1964, Cmnd. 2306.

6 Scottish Advisory Council on Child Care, *Prevention of Neglect in Children* (McBoyle Report), H.M.S.O., March 1963, Cmnd. 1966.

7 Kilbrandon Report, op. cit., p. 99.

8 ibid., p. 95.

9 *Journal of the Royal Society of Health*, Vol. 86, No. 1, Jan.–Feb. 1966, p. 19.

10 ibid., p. 4.

11 Home Office, *The Child, the Family and the Young Offender*, H.M.S.O., August 1965, Cmnd. 2742, p. 4.

12 Seebohm Report, op. cit., p. 11.

13 ibid., p. 18.

14 *Case Conference*, Vol. 12, No. 8, Feb. 1966, p. 214.

15 Sinfield, A., 'Which way for Social Work?', in *The Fifth Social Service*, Fabian Society, 1970, p. 41.

16 *Public Health*, Vol. LXXXII, Sept. 1968, p. 244.

17 *British Medical Journal*, 3.8.68, 3, p. 265.

18 For a case-study illustrating the political importance of juvenile crime as an issue, see Land, H., 'The Development of Detention Centres', in Hall, P. K., Land, H., Parker, R. A. and Webb, A. L., op. cit., pp. 311–70.

19 The Longford Report, op. cit., p. 20.

20 Marris, P. and Rein, M., *Dilemmas of Social Reform*, Routledge and Kegan Paul, 1967, pp. 208–15 and *passim*.

CHAPTER THREE

1 Home Office, op. cit.

2 *Report of the Committee on Housing in Greater London* (Milner Holland Report), H.M.S.O., March 1965, Cmnd. 2605.

3   *Report of the Committee on the Rent Acts* (Francis Report), H.M.S.O., March 1971, Cmnd. 4609.

4   *Report of the Committee into the Impact of Rates on Households* (Allen Report), H.M.S.O., Feb. 1965, Cmnd. 2585.

5   Seebohm Report, op. cit., Chairman's Foreword, p. 3. In an earlier draft his sentiments were expressed more strongly.

6   See Lindblom, C., 'The Science of Muddling Through', *Public Administration Review*, 1959.

7   Seebohm Report, op. cit., Appendix A, p. 241.

8   Family Service Committee Paper (F.S.C.P.) 381 and 472.

9   Seebohm Report, op. cit., p. 34.

10 ibid., p. 21.

11 F.S.C.P. 35. It is discussed in the Seebohm Report, p. 42.

12 F.S.C.P. 83.

13 F.S.C.P. 116. There were many other papers with factual information concerning services administered by the Ministry of Health—but F.S.C.P. 116 contains comment and opinion on the issues raised by the committee.

14 ibid.

15 F.S.C.P. 102.

16 The Seebohm Report, op. cit., pp. 241–2.

17 See S.C.O.S.W. evidence, F.S.C.P. 165, p. 7.

18 F.S.C.P. 231.

19 F.S.C.P. 217.

20 F.S.C.P. 144.

21 F.S.C.P. 210.

22 F.S.C.P. 130.

23 F.S.C.P. 241.

24 F.S.C.P. 127.

25 F.S.C.P. 165, pp. 3–4.

26 F.S.C.P. 95.

27 *Public Health*, Nov. 66–Sept. 67, Vol. LXXX, p. 102.

28 F.S.C.P. 231, p. 6.

29 F.S.C.P. 144, p. 3.

30 F.S.C.P. 165, p. 7.

31 F.S.C.P. 148, p. 4.

32 F.S.C.P. 88, p. 5.

33 F.S.C.P. 183, p. 3.

34 F.S.C.P. 171.

35 F.S.C.P. 84, pp. 1–2.

36 F.S.C.P. 161, p. 1.

37 See, for example, the Younghusband Report, op. cit., pp. 2–3, 311 and *passim* and the Ingleby Report, op. cit., p. 16.

38 The Seebohm Report, op. cit., p. 38.

39 The Seebohm Report, op. cit., p. 41. The study has been deposited

with other material relating to the enquiry in the library of the
Ministry of Housing and Local Government.
40 The Seebohm Report, op. cit., Appendix Q, pp. 347–56.

CHAPTER FOUR
1   Seebohm Report, op. cit., pp. 40–1.
2   ibid., p. 32.
3   ibid., p. 34.
4   F.S.C.P. 251.
5   Seebohm Report, op. cit., p. 111.
6   ibid., p. 119.
7   Central Advisory Council for Education (England), Vol. 1, *Children
    and their Primary Schools* (Plowden Report), November 1966.
8   Seebohm Report, op. cit., p. 61.
9   ibid., pp. 132–4.
10 ibid., p. 211.
11 For discussions of recent development, see: Stevenson, O., *Claimant
    or Client?* Allen and Unwin, 1973. Jordan, B., 'Emergency Payments',
    Social Work Today, 22.2.73, p. 15.
12 Seebohm Report, op. cit., p. 217.
13 *Children and Their Primary Schools*, op. cit., Ch. 5 and *passim.*
14 Ministry of Housing and Local Government, *The Committee on the
    Management of Local Government* (the Maud Committee), H.M.S.O.,
    1967, p. 89.
15 Seebohm Report, op. cit., p. 188.
16 ibid., p. 194.
17 ibid., Appendix F, p. 283.
18 ibid., Appendix F, p. 258.
19 ibid., p. 163.
20 ibid., p. 166.
21 F.S.C.P. 221, p. 7.
22 Seebohm Report, op. cit., p. 209.
23 *Hansard*, Vol. 761, 28.3.68, Col. 309–10.
24 Scottish Home and Health Department, *Social Work and the
    Community*, H.M.S.O., 1966, Cmnd. 3605.
25 Social Work (Scotland) Act, July 1968.
26 Seebohm Report, op. cit., pp. 19 and 193.
27 F.S.C.P. 472.
28 F.S.C.P. 381.
29 *Children and Their Primary Schools*, op. cit., pp. 442–8.
30 Kogan, M., in *The Role of Commissions in Policy-Making*, ed.
    R. Chapman, Allen and Unwin, 1973, p. 102.
31 Seebohm Report, op. cit., p. 16.
32 ibid., p. 16.

CHAPTER FIVE

1   *Report of the Royal Commission on Medical Education* (Todd Report), H.M.S.O., April 1968.

2   *A National Health Service: the administrative structure of the medical and related services in England and Wales*, Ministry of Health, H.M.S.O., 1968.

3   H.C. Deb., Vol. 769, col. 101, written answer.

4   See extracts from Crossman's diaries, *Sunday Times Weekly Review*, for 8 December 1965, 2 March 1975.

5   Private interview.

6   Crossman, R. H. S., *Inside View*, Cape, 1972, pp. 74–5.

7   The *Economist*, 27.7.68, p. 17.

8   *Times Educational Supplement*, July–December 1968, p. 169.

9   *Lancet*, July 1968, p. 201.

10 *British Medical Journal*, 1968, 3, p. 265.

11 *Public Health*, Vol. LXXXI, p. 108.

12 Society of Medical Officers of Health, *Report of the Committee on Local Authority and Allied Personal Social Services, Observations to the Secretary of State.*

13 British Medical Association, *Comments of the Public Health Committee, with an addition by the Central Ethical Committee.*

14 County Councils' Association, *Executive Council Minute*, 11.1.68., p. 2.

15 *Rural District Review*, Appendix to Minutes of Council Meeting, 18.9.68.

16 Donnison, D. V., 'Seebohm—the report and its implications', *Social Work*, Vol. 25, No. 4, Oct. 1968, p. 3.

17 *British Medical Journal*, Supplement, iv, 28.12.68, p. 77.

18 *British Medical Journal*, i, 8.2.69, p. 330.

19 H.C. Deb., Vol. 776, col. 205–6.

20 Private interview.

21 Private interview.

22 H.L. Deb., vol. 298, col. 1193.

23 'Medical Officer of Health or Community Physician?', *Public Health*, Vol. 83, No. 4, May 1969, p. 153.

24 *Times Educational Supplement*, 1.10.69, Jan.–June 1969, p. 70.

25 *Inner London Education Authority, Working Party Report* (Braide Report), June 1969. The report accepted some of the recommendations of an unpublished study of I.L.E.A.'s welfare services finished in 1965. The proposed Education Welfare Service was introduced in October 1970.

26 *Social Work*, Vol. 25, No. 4, p. 35.

27 See, for example, H.C. Deb., vol. 774, cols. 227–8.

28 *Report of the Royal Commission on Local Government in England, 1966–69* (Maud Report), H.M.S.O., June 1969, Cmnd. 4040.

29 H.C. Deb., vol. 787, cols. 435–6.
30 ibid., cols. 2110–11.

CHAPTER SIX

1 H.C. Deb., vol. 790, cols. 631–2.
2 The files of the Society of Medical Officers of Health.
3 See Appendix to the Annual Report of the Council of the B.M.A., *British Medical Journal*, Supplement, ii, 1969, p. 72.
4 *County Council's Association Gazette*, Appendix A, p. 5. Note of meeting between minister and local authority associations, 27.10.69.
5 *C.C.A. Gazette*, op. cit., p. 6.
6 ibid., p. 5.
7 The files of the Standing Conference of Organisations of Social Workers.
8 Welsh Hospital Board, *Report of the Committee of Enquiry*, H.M.S.O., March 1969, Cmnd. 3975.
9 *D.H.S.S.*, Annual Report for the year ending 1969, pp. 42–3.
10 Lady Serota, *Family Health and Social Services in the 70's*, National Institute for Social Work Training, Fourth Eileen Younghusband Lecture, 1970, p. 3.
11 Private correspondence, 18 September 1973.
12 Department of Health and Social Security, *The Future Structure of the National Health Service*, H.M.S.O., 1970.
13 Ministry of Housing and Regional Planning, *Reform of Local Government in England*, H.M.S.O., Feb. 1970, Cmnd. 4276,
14 H.C. Deb., vol. 796, cols. 1406–1520.
15 *H.L. Deb.*, vol. 310, no. 81, 20.5.70.

CHAPTER SEVEN

1 This point is discussed briefly in Chapman, R., *The Role of Commissions in Policy Making*, op. cit., p. 184.
2 Plowden, W., 'The Anatomy of Commissions', *New Society*, Vol. 18, No. 458, p. 105.
3 Chapman, R., op. cit., p. 184.
4 Hall, P., Land, H., Parker, R. and Webb, A. L., *Change, Choice and Conflict in Social Policy*, Heinemann, 1975, pp. 475–509.
5 ibid., pp. 18–20.
6 ibid., p. 176.
7 ibid., p. 179.
8 ibid., p. 486.
9 ibid., p. 483.
10 ibid., p. 499. It was acknowledged that the precise origins of an idea are often extremely difficult to determine. For this reason it may be more useful to think in terms of early advocates of an issue rather than originators.

11   ibid., p. 500.
12   ibid., p. 486.

POSTSCRIPT
 1   Derived from Table 1.3, Klein R. (ed.), *Inflation and Priorities*, Centre for Studies in Social Policy, 1975, p. 14.
 2   Derived from Table 2.11, *Public Expenditure to 1978–79*, Cmnd. 5879, H.M.S.O., 1975, pp. 102–3.

Appendix One

1964

April   Report of the Kilbrandon Committee on *Children and Young Persons in Scotland* published.

June   Report of the Longford Committee on *Crime: A Challenge to Us All* published.

October   Labour Party victory at general election.

1965

April   R. M. Titmuss' speech at the Royal Society of Health Conference, Eastbourne.

May   Ad Hoc Group's Memorandum produced and circulated.

August   Publication of *The Child, the Family and the Young Offender* (Home Office white paper) announcing the establishment of a Committee of Enquiry.

July–December   Chairman and members of the Seebohm Committee selected.

1966

January   First meeting of Seebohm Committee.

April   Douglas Houghton appointed Minister without Portfolio.
Judith Hart leaves the Scottish Office.

May   Warrant given for the establishment of the Royal Commission on Local Government.

August   Richard Crossman becomes Lord President of the Council, Anthony Greenwood becomes Minister of Housing and Local Government.

November   Report of the Plowden Committee on *Children and Their Primary Schools* published.

December   Report of the Mallaby Committee on *Staffing in Local Government* published.

Roy Jenkins replaces Sir Frank Soskice as Home Secretary.

1967
March   Report of the Committee on *Management in Local Government* published.

August   Alice Bacon leaves the Home Office.

Patrick Gordon-Walker becomes Secretary of State for Education.

November   Ministry of Health announces intention to appoint an internal study group on National Health Service reorganization.

1968
April   Publication of *Children in Trouble* (Home Office white paper) and *Report of the Royal Commission on Medical Education* (Todd Report).

Edward Short becomes Secretary of State for Education.

Richard Crossman becomes co-ordinator of the social services.

July   Seebohm Committee Report published.

First green paper on National Health Service Re-organization passed.

Social Work (Scotland) Act passed.

October   Queen's Speech announces government commitment to *Children in Trouble* proposals.

November   Ministry of Social Security and Ministry of Health amalgamated to form the Department of Health and Social Security.

Crossman becomes Secretary of State for Social Services.

December   Decision taken not to allocate the personal social services to one central government department.

1969
January   Lords debate on Seebohm.

White paper on social security.

Seebohm Implementation Action Group formed.

February   Baroness Serota made Junior Minister at the Department of Health and Social Security.

June	*Royal Commission on the Reorganisation of Local Government* published.
	Department of Health and Social Security invites second round of evidence on the Seebohm Committee.
July	Report of the Office of the Lord President of the Council on reactions to the Seebohm Committee produced.
	Cabinet decides to legislate on Seebohm in 1969–70 parliamentary session.
October	Queen's Speech announces government's commitment to Seebohm.
	Interdepartmental group to draft Bill established.
November	*Children and Young Persons Act* passed.
December	Final decisions on the reorganization of the personal social services taken.

1970

February	*Local Authority Social Services Bill* published.
	Second green paper on the reorganization of the N.H.S. published.
	White paper on Local Government Reform published.
May	*Local Authority Social Services Act* passed.
June	General election.

Appendix Two

THE AD HOC GROUP'S MEMORANDUM ON THE
NEED FOR AN ENQUIRY INTO THE
INTEGRATION OF SOCIAL WORK SERVICES
AT THE LOCAL LEVEL

In recent years a series of official committees has studied various aspects of the social work services. These committees have all recognized that many of the problems with which they were concerned were inter-related; each committee, however, was precluded by its terms of reference from considering what this implied. The need for a more comprehensive look at these services has now become urgent for a number of reasons.

Since 1948 there has been a great expansion of services in which social workers are required, particularly in the local authority setting. Major new services have been established in child care and mental health, and important new developments are taking place in work with the physically handicapped and the aged. The ten-year plans for health and welfare services, with their emphasis on prevention and on community care; the responsibilities for preventive work and family service placed on local authorities by the Children and Young Persons Act, 1963; the development of after-care for offenders by the probation service, all indicate that further expansion is certain. In addition, social workers are now being used by general practitioners, and pressure is growing for more welfare officers in housing departments, for social work in schools, for social work amongst immigrants, and for raising the quality of service for a wide range of residential institutions.

The services in which social workers are employed have developed ad hoc in recent years and not in response to any general policy; this may have been inevitable but it is no longer tenable to consider each in isolation. Social workers employed in different services constantly find themselves dealing with the same individuals and with the same families. This overlapping is confusing for the people being helped, uneconomic for the community and frustrating for the social worker.

More serious problems also arise. Different services may develop different or even contradictory policies in work with the same individuals or families. On the other hand, some people may fail to get the services they need. Everybody's business becomes nobody's business. Attempts to co-ordinate services have continued over the last fifteen years but, apart from the diversion of resources involved, the need for special co-ordinating machinery is a sign of weakness in the administrative structure.

The position is at present obscured by the high sense of personal responsibility of most people employed in the social services and gross breakdowns of service rarely occur. Nevertheless, many people fail to get the service they require and evidence of unmet need is increasing. The necessity for a unified approach to people's problems and for continuity of care is now generally accepted but the way in which the services are at present organized makes it difficult to achieve these objectives.

The importance of preventive work has for long been stressed in all contexts, for persons of every age, with all types of physical or mental handicap, of behaviour disorder or of social deviance. Early preventive action is now possible, since many people with serious social difficulties have in fact had some previous contact with social and allied services at the local level. These opportunities for early recognition and help are often missed, however, and this is due, at least partly, to the fragmented structure of the services. When responsibilities overlap no one will regard himself as accountable or can be held accountable.

There is no unified responsibility for the development of social work services at the local level, for attempting to arrive at comprehensive estimates of need as a basis for planning for the future and for the most effective deployment of all available resources. In this situation it is all too possible for policy decisions to be made without sufficient understanding of what is involved and without providing the resources necessary to make the policies a reality.

Social workers increasingly recognize that they are dealing not with specific problems or handicaps but with people, and not only with people in isolation but with people in a social situation, particularly a family situation. As they have gained more understanding and skill in helping people, social workers from different organizations and departments have found themselves providing what is essentially the same type of service. The common basis of social work is affirmed by recent developments in the training of social workers and by the coming together of social workers from different fields of work in the Standing Conference of Organisations of Social Workers.

The problems of staffing also lead to the conclusion that a review of ways in which social workers are recruited and deployed is urgent. At present, there is a very severe shortage of trained social workers and many more will be required if the responsibilities already imposed by legislation are to be met adequately. Even if people of the required calibre were recruited in sufficient numbers, there remain major problems of training and secondment.

The present organization of social work services at the local level hinders the most economic and flexible use of the limited staff available; because the staffing needs of each service are considered in isolation, rational decisions about the deployment and training of social workers cannot be reached.

The expansion of the personal social services, their complexity and the resources involved also underline the need for a high level of professional understanding and skill in the administration of these services. Personnel of the required standard are in short supply and should be used in the most economical and effective way. The training and deployment of administrators of these services cannot be considered apart from the problems of the training and deployment of social workers.

The arguments set out so far are pressing and important because—and only because—they affect the welfare of those whom the services exist to help. The present fragmented organization of services at the community level makes it difficult for the public to use them to the best advantage. This applies especially to the least able and to those in the greatest need.

Many people reach social work service through other services to which they turn in time of trouble—maternity and child welfare clinics, hospitals, general practitioners, schools, courts, housing departments, community centres, the churches, voluntary organizations, welfare officers in industry and other agencies. For these also the present organization of social work services creates difficulties of referral, co-operation and continuity of care; workers in these related fields are often not able to use social services effectively to meet the needs of their clients.

We therefore propose:

1. That an enquiry should be undertaken forthwith into the departmental structure and organization of social work services at the local

level and their relation to other relevant services in the community. The enquiry should be concerned with all the work of local authority children's and welfare departments and with the social work services in local authority departments of health, education and housing; it must also take account of probation and aftercare and social work in hospitals, in the social security services and in relevant voluntary bodies.

2. That the enquiry should be carried out speedily and should not attempt to repeat the special studies already undertaken, or be concerned with wider aspects except insofar as they affect the structure and departmental organization of the services in question. The object would be to recommend changes in structure and organization at the local level which would enable these services to contribute most economically and effectively to the welfare of the community, would allow flexibility for development, and more coherent planning for the future.

The need for such an enquiry is now urgent and of crucial importance. Major developments in social work services are taking place with only incidental consideration of the total position, and this independent development of particular services will make integration still more difficult to achieve in the future. If separate and isolated developments are allowed to continue, the welfare of large numbers of people will be affected adversely, especially the welfare of the most socially handicapped and vulnerable members of the community.

20 May 1965

Appendix Three
Analysis of Members' Initial Views

oo Strongly in favour   o In favour   x Against   xx Strongly against

ISSUES	A	B	C	D	E	F	G	H	I	J
Boundaries of new department										
Including mental health services in s.s.d.	o	o	oo	xx	oo	oo	o	o	o	o
Discouraging a visiting service within the S.B.C.	oo				o				oo	o
Including pre-school provision in s.s.d.	o	o	x		x	o	xx	xx	o	o
Discussing the probation service	o	o	x	x	o	o		x	o	o
Recommending positive discrimination for some areas	o	o	xx		o	o	o	x	o	o
Central/local relationships										
A statutory social services committee	o	o	oo		o	oo	xx	o	o	xx
Ministerial veto over appointment of directors			oo		o	oo	xx	x	o	xx
Ministerial veto over appointments during first 12 months							xx	x		xx
No ministerial veto over appointments	x	o					o	o		o
Timing										
As soon as possible	o	o	o		o	oo	oo	o	o	
Introduction of s.s.d. s to coincide with local government reform				o		oo	oo		oo	oo
Experiment prior to reform						oo				
Specialization										
Emphasis on reduction of specialization within social work		o			o	o	o	x	o	
Training										
Independent training council			oo		o				o	
Government-financed training council					o	oo				

Appendix Four

SEEBOHM IMPLEMENTATION ACTION GROUP
HANDOUT

SEEBOHM — TWO CHEERS

The Government has acted on Seebohm—on the 12th February it published its "Local Authority Social Services Bill". We can applaud the Government for its intention to implement most of Seebohm's recommendations. There is no doubt that they have been influenced by the strength and unity of social worker support for the Seebohm recommendations.

Not all of Seebohm's recommendations have been included in the Bill, as you will see from this check list:—

	Yes	No
Children's Department Services	✓	
Welfare Services for aged and handicapped	✓	
Mental Health Social Work, including residential and day facilities	✓	
Home Help Services	✓	
Other Social Work in Health Departments (e.g. unsupported mothers)	✓	
Education Welfare Services		✓
Housing Welfare Services		✓
A Statutory Local Authority Committee with undivided responsibility	✓	
A Statutory Director of Social Services with undivided responsibility	✓	
A single Central Government Department responsible for the services		✓
A general duty to promote the welfare of the community		✓

It must be remembered that a Bill is not an Act of Parliament and there will be ample opportunity for the opponents of Seebohm to promote amendments while the Bill goes through Parliament.

There will be particular opposition to the inclusion in the Bill of the Mental Health and Home Help Services, while others will argue that these reforms should await the reform of Local Government.

Some opponents of Seebohm will say that the service should not be mandatory on a local authority. It is, therefore, important that we convince Parliament that our clients' needs demand a comprehensive service effective throughout the country (which can only be achieved by mandatory committee and chief officer provisions) as soon as possible. There is no justification for delaying an effective service to thousands of people—the young and the aged—because of reform in the Local Government structure in four or five years' time. On the contrary, with uniform re-organisation now, the social services will be far more ready for Local Government re-organisation when it comes.

MAJOR OMISSIONS
General Duty to promote Social Welfare

It is a matter of concern that the Government has not seen fit to include in the Bill a general provision making it a duty of Local Authorities to promote social welfare in their area (vide. Section 12 Social Work (Scotland) Act, 1968). The Seebohm Report makes it abundantly clear that many minority social problem groups, such as alcoholics, drug addicts, etc., fail to receive adequate help because they do not fit into any neat legal category.

The Schools and Social Work

Seebohm recommended that School Social Work should be the responsibility of the social service department—so did Plowden. And so apparently does the Government, in principle—then why not in the Bill? Powerful Education vested interests should not be allowed to inhibit the clear provision of a comprehensive social service in this vital area of preventive work.

Housing Welfare

The Government apparently accepts the advice of the Central Housing Advisory Committee and of the Seebohm Committee that the social work needs of local authority tenants should not be met by separate Housing Welfare sections but by the Social Services generally, but because few authorities have Housing Welfare sections, the Government does not intend to legislate—we regret that a clearer mandate for Housing Welfare has not been incorporated in the new Bill.

A Countrywide Service

Parliament should delete the clause (15(5)) from the Bill which allows certain areas to be exempted from organising on Seebohm lines. Each part of the country deserves a comprehensive service *now*.

How Many Secretaries of State?

The Bill does not specify which Secretary of State is to carry out the Bill's functions. It could be one of three depending upon the function. How ludicrous can administration get? What opportunities exist here for exercising the usual Local Government formula of "When in doubt—do nothing!" However strong the Bill might be in all other aspects, this could be its death knell.

MAKE SEEBOHM WORK—
ADVOCATE TOTAL SEEBOHM

Appendix Five

LIST OF THOSE INTERVIEWED

As it has not been possible to attribute individually many of the views expressed by those involved in the setting up of the social services departments, a list of those interviewed in connection with this study has been included.

Members of the Seebohm Committee
(as described in their report).

Frederic Seebohm, Esq.   Baroness Serota
R. Huws Jones, Esq.   Professor J. N. Morris
Dr R. A. Parker   M. F. Simson, Esq.
P. Leonard, Esq.   W. E. Lane, Esq.
Lady James of Rusholme

Ministers
(the office refers to that held when the individual concerned was involved in the policy developments discussed here).

Rt. Hon. R. H. S. Crossman, Secretary of State for the Social Services
Mr D. Houghton, Co-ordinator of the Social Services
Miss A. Bacon, Minister of State (Home Office)
Mrs J. Hart, Minister of State (Scottish Office)

Civil Servants

Mr J. Pater, Assistant Under Secretary (Ministry of Health)
Mr P. Oglesby, Private Secretary to Douglas Houghton
Mr G. Otton, Assistant Under Secretary (Home Office)
Mr M. Russell, Assistant Secretary (Home Office)
Miss J. Cooper, Assistant Secretary (Home Office)
Miss A. Sheridan, Assistant Secretary (Ministry of Health)
Mr P. R. Odgers, Senior civil servant (Office of the Lord President of the Council)

Influential Individuals and Members of Pressure Groups

Professor R. M. Titmuss, member of Judith Hart's Advisory Group
Mr D. Jones, Deputy Director of the National Institute for Social Work Training
Dame Eileen Younghusband
Dr T. White, member of the Association of Child Care Officers and leading member of the Seebohm Implementation Action Group
Mrs K. McDougall, Chairman of the Standing Conference of Organisations of Social Workers
Representative of the Association of Municipal Corporations
Representative of the County Councils' Association
Representative of the Society of Medical Officers of Health

Scotland

Mrs K. Carmichael, member of Judith Hart's Advisory Group
Mr J. O. Johnston
Miss M. Brown, Department of Social Administration, Edinburgh University
Mr A. Rowe

Index

1. *The Report of the Committee on Local Authority and Allied Social Services is referred to throughout as 'Seebohm'.*
2. *Acts of Parliament will be found together under Acts.*
3. *'Committee' (unspecified) means the Seebohm Committee.*

153

Aves, G. M., 23n

Bacon, Alice, 19n, 21–2, 25–6, 37, 140, 151
Barratt, Sir Charles, 30
Beneficiaries under Social Services Departments, table of, 123
Birk, Alma, 16n
Bowlby, John, 16n
British Association of Social Workers, 130
British Federation of Social Workers, 11–12
British Medical Association, 42, 58, 64
    evidence to committee, 52–3
    reaction to report, 87, 90–1, 94, 96, 99–100, 109
British Medical Journal, 32, 86, 91
Brooke, Baroness, 93
Brown, M., 152

Cabinet discussions on Committee proposals, 82, 96, 103n, 141
Callaghan, James, 83, 96–7, 98
Cardiff, Ely Hospital enquiry at, 104–5
Carmichael, K., 152
Central Council for Education and Training in Social Work, 89n, 127
Central and Local Government:
    committee's decisions as to responsibilities of, 68–70, 103–4
    committee members' initial views, 146
    rivalries between, 112
Central Training Council in Child Care, 71, 89
Change, Choice and Conflict (Hall *et al.*), 117–21
Change, community pressure for, 1–18:
    A Family Service?, 16–17
    common identity amongst social workers, 11–14
    co-ordination or re-organization?, 14–15
    inadequate planning machinery, 9
    new approach, 9–11
    1948 service, structure of, 3–7:
        deprived children, 3–4
        health and welfare, 4–7
        observations, 17–18
    welfare services:
        growth of, 7–9
        one agency or several?, 1–3
Chief Officer posts, 69, 88 and n, 124
Child, The, the Family and the Young Offender (Home Office), 37, 133, 139
Child guidance, 7, 16, 75, 99
Child Poverty Group, 92
Children:
    as beneficiaries under social services, 123
    preventing crime by, 10
    see also Juvenile crime